THE COMFORTING DASH DIET COOKBOOK FOR BEGINNERS 2024

Easy and Delicious Low-Sodium Recipes
to Combat Hypertension and Regain the Health You Desire

Olympia Grayson

Copyright 2024 - All rights reserved.

Permission to reproduce, distribute, or transmit the content of this book in any form is strictly prohibited without express written consent from the author or publisher. Neither the author nor the publisher will be held liable for any damages, compensations, or monetary losses arising from the information presented in this book, whether direct or indirect.

Legal Statement:

This publication is protected by copyright laws. It is intended solely for personal consumption. Without the explicit approval of the author or publisher, no part of this book's content may be modified, shared, sold, utilized, cited, or paraphrased.

Disclaimer:

The content in this document is provided for educational and entertainment purposes only. While all efforts have been made to ensure the information is accurate, timely, and reliable, no guarantees or warranties are given or implied. The author does not provide legal, financial, medical, or any professional counsel through this book. The information herein has been sourced from various places. Before implementing any strategies mentioned in this book, it is advised to seek counsel from a qualified professional.

By engaging with this material, the reader acknowledges that the author is not liable for any losses, whether direct or indirect, stemming from the information in this document, including any errors, omissions, or inaccuracies.

Table of Contents

INTRODUCTION 9
  WHAT IS THE DASH DIET? 9
  KEY MOTIVATIONS FOR ADOPTING THE DASH DIET TO IMPROVE YOUR WELL-BEING 10
  BENEFITS OF THE DASH DIET FOR HEALTH IN GENERAL, HYPERTENSION CONTROL, AND WEIGHT MANAGEMENT 11
  SODIUM AND ITS IMPACT ON HEALTH 12

CHAPTER 1. PLANNING YOUR DASH DIET MEALS 14
  SETTING YOUR GOALS 14
  CREATING A BALANCED PLATE AND CONTROLLING PORTION SIZES 14
  TIPS FOR SUCCESSFULLY FOLLOWING THE DASH DIET EVEN WHEN YOU NEED TO EAT AT A RESTAURANT 15
  FOOD TO EAT 16
  FOOD TO AVOID 16
  UNDERSTANDING NUTRITIONAL LABELS 17
  SHOPPING LISTS 17

CHAPTER 2. BREAKFAST RECIPES 21
  2. QUINOA BREAKFAST BOWL 21
  3. OATMEAL WITH MIXED BERRIES 21
  4. BERRY AND SPINACH SMOOTHIE 21
  5. SWEET POTATO AND SPINACH HASH 22
  6. VEGGIE BREAKFAST BURRITO 22
  7. TOFU SCRAMBLE 22
  8. BLUEBERRY AND ALMOND OVERNIGHT OATS 23
  9. PEANUT BUTTER AND BANANA OATMEAL 23
  10. VEGGIE AND HUMMUS WRAP 24
  11. RASPBERRY AND ALMOND CHIA PUDDING 24
  12. MIXED BERRY SMOOTHIE 24
  13. CINNAMON AND APPLE OATMEAL 25
  14. VEGGIE AND QUINOA BREAKFAST BOWL 25
  15. ALMOND AND BANANA TOAST 25
  16. TOMATO AND BASIL OMELET 26

CHAPTER 4. SMOOTHIES AND SHAKES RECIPES 27
  18. BERRY BLAST SMOOTHIE 27
  19. GREEN POWER SMOOTHIE 27
  20. TROPICAL DELIGHT SMOOTHIE 27
  21. CINNAMON APPLE SMOOTHIE 28
  22. CARROT CAKE SMOOTHIE 28
  23. CITRUS KALE SMOOTHIE 28
  24. POMEGRANATE BLUEBERRY SHAKE 29
  25. CHERRY ALMOND SMOOTHIE 29
  26. AVOCADO KALE SMOOTHIE 29
  27. MANGO SPINACH SMOOTHIE 30
  28. RASPBERRY OATMEAL SMOOTHIE 30
  29. PEACH ALMOND SMOOTHIE 30
  30. SPINACH AND PINEAPPLE SMOOTHIE 30
  31. BLUEBERRY CHIA SEED SHAKE 31
  32. BANANA KIWI SMOOTHIE 31

CHAPTER 6. SNACKS RECIPES 32

- 34. Hummus and Veggie Sticks 32
- 35. Edamame with Lemon and Sea Salt 32
- 36. Avocado and Salsa Dip 32
- 37. Grilled Vegetable Salad 32
- 38. Cherry Tomatoes with Balsamic Glaze 33
- 39. Spinach and Tomato Frittata 33
- 40. Hard-Boiled Eggs with Mustard 34
- 41. Bell Pepper and Guacamole Bites 34
- 42. Crispy Baked Zucchini Chips 34
- 43. Mango and Coconut Chia Pudding 35
- 44. Tuna and Cucumber Boats 35
- 45. Cauliflower Popcorn 35
- 46. Watermelon and Mint Skewers 36
- 47. Quinoa Salad 36
- 48. Chia Pudding with Berries 36

CHAPTER 8. SAUCE AND SPICE-BASED SEASONINGS RECIPES TO NOT MISS THE SALT ON FOODS 38

- 50. Lemon Herb Sauce 38
- 51. Garlic and Herb Seasoning 38
- 52. Ginger Sesame Dressing 38
- 53. Chili-Lime Seasoning 38
- 54. Balsamic Dijon Vinaigrette 39
- 55. Turmeric and Cumin Seasoning 39
- 56. Lemon Pepper Seasoning 39
- 57. Rosemary Dijon Marinade 40
- 58. Lemon Basil Pesto 40
- 59. Spicy Tomato Salsa 40
- 60. Cumin-Lime Dressing 41
- 61. Basil Tomato Sauce 41
- 62. Lemon Dill Dressing 41
- 63. Mediterranean Herb Blend 41
- 64. Sesame Ginger Sauce 42

CHAPTER 10. SALADS RECIPES 43

- 66. Lemon Herb Quinoa Salad 43
- 67. Mediterranean Lentil Salad 43
- 68. Tuna and White Bean Salad 44
- 69. Asian-Inspired Edamame Salad 44
- 70. Spinach and Strawberry Salad 45
- 71. Black Bean and Corn Salad 45
- 72. Spinach and Chickpea Salad with Lemon Tahini Dressing 46
- 73. Caprese Salad with Balsamic Glaze 46
- 74. Spinach and Avocado Salad with Cilantro Lime Dressing 46
- 75. Mediterranean Chickpea Salad 47
- 76. Roasted Sweet Potato and Kale Salad 47
- 77. Waldorf Salad with Greek Yogurt Dressing 48
- 78. Roasted Beet and Orange Salad 48
- 79. Spinach and Pear Salad with Dijon Vinaigrette 49
- 80. Broccoli and Chickpea Salad with Lemon Garlic Dressing 50

CHAPTER 12. POULTRY RECIPES 51

- 82. Baked Herb-Crusted Turkey Brest 51
- 83. Citrus-Marinated Grilled Chicken 51
- 84. Herbed Chicken Stir-Fry 51
- 85. Cilantro Lime Chicken Tenders 52
- 86. Rosemary Dijon Chicken 52
- 87. Ginger Sesame Chicken Stir-Fry 52
- 88. Paprika Chicken with Roasted Vegetables 53
- 89. Honey Mustard Chicken with Steamed Asparagus 53
- 90. Tomato Basil Chicken 53
- 91. Curry Chicken with Cauliflower Rice 54
- 92. Herb-Crusted Chicken with Sautéed Spinach 54
- 93. Teriyaki Chicken with Broccoli 55
- 94. Almond-Crusted Chicken Tenders 55
- 95. Pineapple Teriyaki Chicken 55
- 96. Spicy Cajun Chicken with Sautéed Spinach 56

CHAPTER 14. BEEF RECIPES 57

- 98. Beef Stir-Fry with Broccoli and Bell Peppers 57
- 99. Beef and Vegetable Kabobs 57
- 100. Beef and Spinach Salad 57
- 101. Beef and Mushroom Stuffed Bell Peppers 58
- 102. Beef and Asparagus Stir-Fry 58
- 103. Beef and Bean Chili 59
- 104. Beef and Spinach Stuffed Portobello Mushrooms 59
- 105. Beef and Green Bean Stir-Fry 60
- 106. Beef and Eggplant Skillet 60
- 107. Beef and Pea Risotto 60
- 108. Beef and Mushroom Lettuce Wraps 61
- 109. Beef and Cucumber Salad 61
- 110. Beef and Sweet Potato Hash 62
- 111. Beef and Tomato Quinoa Bowl 62
- 112. Beef and Cauliflower Rice Bowl 63

CHAPTER 16. VEGETABLES AND GRAINS RECIPES 64

- 114. Lentil and Vegetable Soup 64
- 115. Quinoa-Stuffed Bell Peppers 64
- 116. Mushroom and Spinach Risotto 65
- 117. Roasted Veggie and Chickpea Bowl 65
- 118. Brown Rice and Vegetable Stir-Fry 66
- 119. Spinach and Mushroom Oatmeal 66
- 120. Greek Salad 67
- 121. Cauliflower and Chickpea Curry 67
- 122. Zucchini Noodles with Tomato Sauce 67
- 123. Spaghetti Squash Primavera 68
- 124. Cabbage and Black Bean Tacos 68
- 125. Sweet Potato and Chickpea Hash 69
- 126. Quinoa and Asparagus Salad 69

127. Stuffed Portobello Mushrooms 70
128. Millet and Roasted Vegetable Salad 71

CHAPTER 18. FISH AND SHELLFISH RECIPES 72

130. Baked Salmon with Dill 72
131. Poached Tilapia with Herbed Tomatoes 72
132. Baked Herb-Crusted Snapper 72
133. Grilled Swordfish with Herb Salsa 73
134. Garlic and Herb Baked Scallops 73
135. Shrimp and Vegetable Stir-Fry 73
136. Lemon Dill Baked Catfish 74
137. Baked Lemon Garlic Tilapia 74
138. Grilled Tuna Steak with Cucumber Salad 75
139. Baked Garlic Butter Shrimp 75
140. Sesame Crusted Salmon with Spinach 75
141. Mediterranean Style Grilled Sardines 76
142. Broiled Lemon Butter Lobster Tails 76
143. Seared Scallops with Spinach 76
144. Baked Coconut Shrimp 77

CHAPTER 20. SIDE RECIPES 78

146. Lemon Herb Quinoa 78
147. Garlic Roasted Brussels Sprouts 78
148. Roasted Asparagus 78
149. Brown Rice Pilaf 79
150. Steamed Green Beans with Almonds 79
151. Stir-Fried Broccoli and Mushrooms 79
152. Sautéed Spinach with Garlic 80
153. Herbed Brown Lentils 80
154. Grilled Eggplant 81
155. Sautéed Snow Peas with Lemon 81
156. Roasted Red Pepper Hummus 81
157. Cauliflower "Mashed Potatoes" 82
158. Sautéed Swiss Chard 82
159. Roasted Cauliflower with Turmeric 82
160. Avocado and Tomato Salad 83

CHAPTER 22. SOUPS RECIPES 84

162. Vegetable Quinoa Soup 84
163. Chickpea and Vegetable Soup 84
164. Broccoli and White Bean Soup 84
165. Spinach and Mushroom Soup 85
166. Asparagus and Lemon Soup 85
167. Sweet Potato and Black Bean Soup 85
168. Cauliflower and Turmeric Soup 86
169. Green Pea and Mint Soup 86
170. Spinach and Red Lentil Soup 87
171. Zucchini and Basil Soup 87

- 172. CARROT AND GINGER SOUP 87
- 173. SPICY BELL PEPPER SOUP 88
- 174. EGGPLANT AND TOMATO SOUP 88
- 175. ARTICHOKE AND SPINACH SOUP 88
- 176. GREEN BEAN AND ALMOND SOUP 89

CHAPTER 24. DESSERTS RECIPES 90

- 178. BAKED APPLES WITH CINNAMON 90
- 179. PINEAPPLE AND BANANA SORBET 90
- 180. CHOCOLATE AVOCADO MOUSSE 90
- 181. CINNAMON BAKED PEARS 91
- 182. MANGO AND RASPBERRY FROZEN YOGURT 91
- 183. FRUIT SALAD WITH HONEY-LIME DRIZZLE 91
- 184. PEACH AND BLUEBERRY CRISP 92
- 185. APRICOT AND ALMOND RICE PUDDING 92
- 186. COCONUT AND MANGO CHIA POPSICLES 92
- 187. BAKED BANANA WITH CINNAMON AND WALNUTS 93
- 188. FROZEN YOGURT BARK 93
- 189. MINTY WATERMELON SLUSH 93
- 190. POMEGRANATE AND KIWI FRUIT SALAD 94
- 191. CRANBERRY AND WALNUT QUINOA 94
- 192. PEACH AND RASPBERRY SMOOTHIE 94

CHAPTER 26. BONUS #1 TASTY AND QUICK INSTANT POT RECIPES FOR DELICIOUS LUNCHES AND DINNERS 96

- 194. INSTANT POT QUINOA AND BLACK BEAN BOWL 96
- 195. INSTANT POT CHICKPEA CURRY 96
- 196. INSTANT POT MINESTRONE SOUP 96
- 197. INSTANT POT RED LENTIL CURRY 97
- 198. INSTANT POT BLACK-EYED PEA STEW 97
- 199. INSTANT POT MOROCCAN CHICKPEA STEW 98
- 200. INSTANT POT BROWN RICE AND BEAN BOWL 98
- 201. INSTANT POT SPINACH AND LENTIL CURRY 99
- 202. INSTANT POT VEGETABLE AND CHICKPEA CURRY 99
- 203. INSTANT POT BLACK BEAN AND CORN SOUP 99
- 204. INSTANT POT TOMATO AND LENTIL SOUP 100
- 205. INSTANT POT SPINACH AND MUSHROOM RISOTTO 100
- 206. INSTANT POT MEDITERRANEAN QUINOA SALAD 101
- 207. INSTANT POT SWEET POTATO AND LENTIL STEW 101
- 208. INSTANT POT RATATOUILLE 101
- 209. INSTANT POT LEMON HERB RICE WITH ASPARAGUS 102
- 210. INSTANT POT BLACK BEAN AND QUINOA STUFFED PEPPERS 102
- 211. INSTANT POT CILANTRO LIME RICE WITH BLACK BEANS 103
- 212. INSTANT POT BUTTERNUT SQUASH SOUP 103
- 213. INSTANT POT MEXICAN RICE WITH PINTO BEANS 103

CHAPTER 28. BONUS #2 EASY AND DELICIOUS MEAL PREPS FOR VERY BUSY PEOPLE WHO ARE OFTEN OUT FOR WORK 105

- 215. QUINOA AND VEGETABLE STIR-FRY 105
- 216. CHICKPEA AND SPINACH CURRY 105

217. Spinach and Mushroom Frittata 105
218. Cauliflower Rice Bowl 106
219. Salmon and Asparagus Foil Pack 106
220. Eggplant and Chickpea Curry 106
221. Spaghetti Squash with Tomato Sauce 107
222. Mushroom and Spinach Stuffed Bell Peppers 107
223. Roasted Vegetable and Quinoa Bowl 107
224. Chickpea and Vegetable Stir-Fry 108
225. Cucumber and Tomato Salad 108
226. Sweet Potato and Black Bean Hash 108
227. Mango and Black Bean Salad 109
228. Tofu and Vegetable Stir-Fry 109
229. Cauliflower and Broccoli Salad 109
230. Mushroom and Spinach Omelet 110
231. Tofu and Vegetable Curry 110
232. Lemon Garlic Roasted Brussels Sprouts 111
233. Cabbage and Carrot Slaw 111
234. Baked Sweet Potatoes with Salsa 111

30-DAY MEAL PLAN 112

CONCLUSION 116

MEASUREMENT CONVERSION CHART 117

INDEX 119

INTRODUCTION

In a world where many people are looking for quick fixes and trendy diets, the DASH Diet stands out as a reliable and healthy choice. DASH, short for Dietary Approaches to Stop Hypertension, is a well-known eating plan that can help improve your overall health, manage high blood pressure, and assist with weight control. It's based on scientific research and trusted by medical experts. The DASH Diet provides a holistic way to feed your body while reducing the risks associated with eating too much sodium.

What is the DASH Diet?

The DASH diet is a dietary plan that was originally developed by the National Heart, Lung, & Blood Institute (NHLBI) to help individuals manage and prevent high blood pressure, also known as hypertension. Over time, it has evolved into a well-rounded dietary pattern that is recommended for promoting overall health and well-being.

At its core, the DASH diet encourages the consumption of a wide variety of nutrient-rich foods while limiting the intake of certain items known to contribute to high blood pressure and other health issues. It emphasizes the following key components:

- **Fruits and Vegetables:** The DASH diet encourages a generous intake of fruits and vegetables, which are rich in essential vitamins, minerals, fiber, and antioxidants. These components not only help reduce blood pressure but also provide numerous health benefits.
- **Whole Grains:** Choose foods like brown rice, whole wheat bread, and quinoa over processed grains because they have more fiber & are digested more slowly. This can keep your blood sugar steady and lower your chances of heart problems.
- **Lean Proteins:** Lean protein sources such as poultry, fish, beans, and legumes are staples of the DASH diet. These foods offer vital amino acids without the saturated fats present in red meats.
- **Dairy:** Low-fat or fat-free dairy products like milk, yogurt, and cheese are encouraged to meet calcium and protein needs while minimizing saturated fat intake.
- **Nuts, Seeds, and Legumes:** These healthy foods are packed with good fats, protein, and fiber, which are all great for your heart and keeping you feeling full.

- **Fats and Oils:** The DASH diet recommends limited consumption of fats and oils, with an emphasis on heart-healthy fats like those found in olive oil, avocados, and nuts.
- **Sweets and Added Sugars:** Sweets and added sugars should be consumed sparingly, as they can contribute to weight gain and increase the risk of chronic diseases like diabetes and heart disease.
- **Sodium Restriction:** One of the most critical aspects of the DASH diet is the reduction of sodium (salt) intake, as excessive sodium consumption is a known contributor to high blood pressure.

Key Motivations for Adopting the DASH Diet to Improve Your Well-being

Adopting the DASH diet can be a life-changing decision with numerous motivations behind it. Here are some reasons why individuals choose to embrace this dietary approach:

1. **Reduced Sodium Intake**

The DASH diet recommends reducing sodium (salt) intake, which can help lower the risk of high blood pressure and related health problems. Lowering sodium intake can also reduce the risk of fluid retention and bloating.

2. **Balanced and Sustainable**

In contrast to certain trendy diets that prove challenging to maintain over the long haul, the DASH diet stands out as a well-balanced and enduring dietary approach. It promotes the inclusion of diverse foods from all food groups, which facilitates long-term adherence.

3. **Flexibility**

The DASH diet is flexible and can be adapted to suit different dietary preferences and cultural backgrounds. Whether you're a vegetarian, vegan, or have specific dietary restrictions, you can customize the DASH diet to meet your needs while still reaping its health benefits.

4. **Lifestyle Improvement**

Adopting the DASH diet often goes hand-in-hand with other healthy lifestyle changes, such as regular physical activity and reduced sodium intake. These combined efforts can lead to significant improvements in overall well-being.

5. **Better Overall Eating Habits**

The DASH diet encourages mindful eating and a focus on whole, unprocessed foods. By following this dietary approach, you can develop better eating habits that promote long-term well-being.

6. **Positive Mental Health**

Consuming a healthy and balanced diet can positively affect your mental well-being. Nutrient-rich foods can help stabilize mood, increase energy levels, and support cognitive function, contributing to an overall sense of well-being.

7. **Enhanced Energy Levels**

The DASH diet encourages the consumption of complex carbohydrates from sources like whole grains and legumes. These foods offer a consistent energy supply, reducing the likelihood of energy fluctuations that are commonly linked to refined carbohydrates and sugary snacks.

Benefits of the DASH Diet for Health in General, Hypertension Control, and Weight Management

The DASH diet offers a myriad of benefits that extend beyond its primary focus on hypertension control. Let's explore these advantages in detail:

1. **Blood Pressure Control:** The most well-established benefit of the DASH diet is its ability to lower blood pressure. Research consistently demonstrates that people who adhere to the DASH diet consistently experience notable decreases in both systolic and diastolic blood pressure readings. This reduction is attributed to the diet's potassium-rich foods, which help counteract the effects of sodium and relax blood vessel walls. By adopting the DASH diet, individuals with hypertension can potentially reduce their reliance on medication and improve their overall cardiovascular health.

2. **Heart Disease Prevention:** Heart disease remains a leading cause of death globally, making preventive measures crucial. The DASH diet, with its emphasis on reducing saturated fats and cholesterol, contributes to heart disease prevention by lowering the risk of atherosclerosis (hardening of the arteries) and subsequent heart attacks.

3. **Weight Loss and Maintenance:** For individuals aiming to lose extra weight or keep a healthy weight, the DASH diet provides a practical and successful method. By promoting the consumption of nutrient-dense foods and controlling portion sizes, it helps individuals create a calorie deficit necessary for weight loss. Furthermore, the diet's balance of macronutrients supports muscle retention and metabolic health.

4. **Improved Insulin Sensitivity:** The DASH diet's focus on whole grains, lean proteins, and low-sugar foods can improve insulin sensitivity, making it a valuable dietary approach for

individuals with prediabetes or type 2 diabetes. Stable blood sugar levels contribute to better energy management & reduce the risk of diabetes-related complications.

5. **Lowered Risk of Stroke:** Stroke is another life-threatening condition associated with hypertension. Following the DASH diet can significantly reduce the risk of stroke by addressing hypertension and promoting overall cardiovascular health.

6. **Reduced Cancer Risk:** Although it's not primarily designed as a cancer prevention diet, the DASH diet's focus on fruits and vegetables, which are packed with antioxidants, can play a role in lowering the risk of specific types of cancer. Antioxidants work to counteract harmful free radicals in the body, which can decrease cell damage and the likelihood of cancer formation.

7. **Digestive Health:** The DASH diet's fiber-rich components, such as whole grains, fruits, and vegetables, support healthy digestion. Adequate fiber intake promotes regular bowel movements, reduces the risk of constipation, and may lower the risk of gastrointestinal conditions, such as diverticulosis.

8. **Enhanced Longevity:** By addressing various aspects of health, including blood pressure, heart disease, and weight management, the DASH diet has the potential to extend an individual's lifespan. Long-term adherence to the DASH diet can lead to a healthier, more vibrant life.

Sodium and its Impact on Health

Sodium, a crucial electrolyte, plays a significant role in maintaining the body's fluid balance, nerve function, and muscle contractions. However, excessive sodium intake is linked to various health issues, particularly hypertension. Here's how sodium impacts health:

- **Hypertension:** High sodium intake is a primary contributor to hypertension. When you consume too much sodium, your body retains water to dilute the excess, increasing blood volume and leading to higher blood pressure. Over time, this can damage blood vessels and contribute to the development of heart disease and stroke.

- **Kidney Function:** The kidneys play a vital role in regulating sodium levels in the body. Excess sodium puts additional strain on the kidneys, potentially leading to kidney disease or exacerbating existing kidney conditions.

- **Fluid Balance:** Sodium helps regulate the body's fluid balance. Excessive sodium intake can disrupt this balance, leading to swelling (edema) and fluid retention, which can be uncomfortable and increase the risk of high blood pressure.
- **Bone Health:** Some studies suggest that high sodium intake may be linked to lower bone density. Excessive sodium can lead to the loss of calcium through urine, potentially weakening bones over time.
- **Stomach Cancer:** While the link is not fully understood, some research has suggested that high-sodium diets may be associated with an increased risk of stomach cancer.

Given these potential health risks, it's crucial to be mindful of sodium intake and make informed dietary choices. The DASH diet addresses this by limiting sodium intake to a recommended level of 2,300 milligrams (mg) per day, with an ideal target of 1,500 mg for individuals with hypertension or at risk of developing it. This sodium restriction is achieved by reducing the consumption of processed and salty foods while increasing the intake of fresh, whole foods.

CHAPTER 1. PLANNING YOUR DASH DIET MEALS

Meal planning is a crucial step in successfully adopting the DASH diet. This dietary approach emphasizes nutrient-rich foods, portion control, and sodium reduction to promote overall health and control hypertension. In this chapter, we will discuss the essential aspects of planning your DASH diet meals.

Setting Your Goals

Before you start planning your DASH diet meals, it's essential to set clear and realistic goals. Your goals will serve as a roadmap for your dietary journey and help you stay motivated. Here are some common DASH diet goals:

1. **Blood Pressure Control:** If you have hypertension or want to prevent it, your primary goal may be to lower or maintain healthy blood pressure levels.
2. **Weight Management:** If weight management is your focus, set specific weight loss or maintenance goals that align with your health objectives.
3. **Overall Health Improvement:** Many people adopt the DASH diet to improve their overall health, including reducing the risk of chronic diseases & increasing energy levels.
4. **Disease Prevention:** If you have specific health conditions like diabetes or heart disease, tailor your goals to managing or preventing those conditions.
5. **Lifestyle Adjustment:** The DASH diet can be a long-term lifestyle change. Your goal may be to make sustainable dietary changes that you can maintain for the rest of your life.

Creating a Balanced Plate and Controlling Portion Sizes

The DASH diet encourages a balanced plate that includes a variety of nutrient-rich foods. Here's a general guideline for creating your DASH diet plate:

1. **Fruits & Vegetables:** Make sure half of your plate is filled with a variety of colorful fruits and veggies. They're packed with important vitamins, minerals, and antioxidants.
2. **Grains:** Reserve a quarter of your plate for whole grains such as whole wheat pasta, brown rice, or quinoa. These grains offer fiber and help maintain steady blood sugar levels.
3. **Lean Proteins:** The remaining one-quarter of your plate can be lean protein sources such as poultry, fish, beans, or legumes. These foods provide essential amino acids without excessive saturated fats.

4. **Dairy:** Include low-fat or fat-free dairy products like milk, yogurt, or cheese as a side or as part of your meal.
5. **Nuts, Seeds, and Legumes:** These can be incorporated into your meals or snacks for added nutrients and healthy fats.
6. **Fats and Oils:** Use healthy fats like olive oil, avocados, or nuts sparingly for cooking or as salad dressings.
7. **Sweets and Added Sugars:** Limit sweets and added sugars to occasional treats.

Controlling portion sizes is also crucial to achieving your DASH diet goals. Pay attention to recommended serving sizes and consider using measuring tools to help you portion your food accurately.

Tips for Successfully Following the DASH Diet Even When You Need to Eat at a Restaurant

Maintaining the DASH diet while dining out can be challenging, but it's possible with some thoughtful choices. Here are some tips to help you stick to your DASH diet when eating at a restaurant:

1. **Research Ahead of Time:** Check the restaurant's menu online prior to going. Look for DASH-friendly options like salads, grilled proteins, and dishes with lots of vegetables.
2. **Customize Your Order:** Don't be afraid to customize your order. Ask for substitutions like steamed vegetables instead of fried sides and request sauces or dressings on the side so you can control the amount.
3. **Choose Grilled or Baked:** Opt for grilled or baked proteins instead of fried options. This reduces saturated fat intake.
4. **Limit Sodium:** Ask for dishes with less salt or request that the chef go easy on the salt. You can also try to remove salty condiments or toppings.
5. **Watch Portions:** Restaurant servings are often larger than necessary. Consider sharing an entree with a dining companion or ask for a to-go container to pack up half of your meal prior to you start eating.
6. **Beware of Hidden Calories:** Be cautious of calorie-dense dishes that may appear healthy but are loaded with hidden fats, sugars, or excessive calories.

7. **Stay Hydrated:** Choose water, herbal tea, or other low-calorie beverages instead of sugary sodas or excessive amounts of alcohol.
8. **Ask Questions:** Don't hesitate to ask your server about ingredients, preparation methods, and portion sizes if you're uncertain about a menu item.

Food to Eat

The DASH diet promotes the intake of a diverse range of nutrient-rich foods. Here's a list of foods to include in your DASH diet:

- **Fruits:** Apples, oranges, berries, bananas, and all types of fruits are excellent choices due to their rich vitamin and antioxidant content.
- **Vegetables:** Leafy greens, broccoli, carrots, bell peppers, and other colorful vegetables provide essential nutrients and fiber.
- **Whole Grains:** Brown rice, quinoa, oats, whole wheat pasta, and whole grain bread are high in fiber and nutrients.
- **Lean Proteins:** Choose poultry, fish, beans, lentils, tofu, and other sources of lean protein. These options are low in saturated fat.
- **Dairy:** Choose low-fat or fat-free dairy items like milk, yogurt, and cheese to fulfill your calcium requirements.
- **Nuts and Seeds:** Almonds, chia seeds, walnuts, and flaxseeds are healthy sources of fats, protein, and fiber.
- **Legumes:** Peas, lentils, and beans are rich in fiber and protein, making them excellent choices for DASH meals.
- **Healthy Fats:** Include avocados, olive oil, and nuts in your diet for heart-healthy fats.
- **Herbs and Spices:** Use herbs & spices like basil, oregano, garlic, and cinnamon to flavor your dishes without adding sodium.

Food to Avoid

To successfully follow the DASH diet, it's essential to limit or avoid certain foods that can contribute to high blood pressure & other health issues. Here's a list of foods to limit or avoid:

- **Sodium-rich Foods:** Decrease your intake of high-sodium foods such as processed meats, canned soups, fast food, and salty snacks.
- **Sugary Beverages:** Limit or eliminate sugary sodas, fruit juices, and sweetened drinks.

- **Sweets and Added Sugars:** Minimize consumption of sweets, candies, and foods with excessive added sugars.
- **Highly Processed Foods:** Avoid highly processed and packaged foods, as they often contain unhealthy fats, added sugars, and excessive sodium.
- **Fried Foods:** Cut back on fried foods, which are often high in unhealthy fats.
- **Red Meat:** Limit red meat consumption, especially processed red meats like bacon and sausages.

Understanding Nutritional Labels

It's crucial to grasp how to interpret nutritional labels when you're following the DASH diet. These labels offer valuable insights into the nutritional composition of packaged foods. Here are key components to pay attention to on nutritional labels:

1. **Serving Size:** Pay attention to the serving size, as all the nutritional information on the label is based on this portion.
2. **Calories:** Check the calorie count to make informed choices about portion sizes.
3. **Sodium:** Look for the sodium content and choose lower-sodium options whenever possible.
4. **Total Fat:** Assess the total fat content and aim for products with lower amounts of saturated and trans fats.
5. **Fiber:** Seek products with higher fiber content, as fiber is an essential component of the DASH diet.
6. **Sugars:** Be mindful of added sugars, and choose products with minimal added sugar content.
7. **Ingredients:** Review the ingredient list to identify any unhealthy additives, preservatives, or high-sodium ingredients.

Shopping Lists

Fruits:
- Apples
- Bananas
- Oranges
- Berries (strawberries, blueberries, raspberries)

- Grapes
- Melons (watermelon, cantaloupe)
- Citrus fruits (grapefruits, lemons, limes)
- Peaches
- Pears
- Kiwi

Vegetables:

- Leafy greens (spinach, kale, collard greens)
- Carrots
- Broccoli
- Cauliflower
- Tomatoes
- Bell peppers (red, green, yellow)
- Cucumbers
- Zucchini
- Brussels sprouts
- Sweet potatoes

Whole Grains:

- Brown rice
- Quinoa
- Oats
- Whole wheat pasta
- Whole grain bread
- Barley
- Farro
- Whole grain cereal

Protein:

- Lean cuts of poultry (chicken, turkey)
- Lean cuts of beef or pork (occasionally and in moderation)
- Fish (salmon, tuna, trout)

- Shellfish (shrimp, crab)
- Tofu
- Legumes (beans, lentils, chickpeas)
- Nuts (almonds, walnuts)
- Seeds (flaxseeds, chia seeds)

Dairy and Dairy Alternatives:
- Low-fat or fat-free yogurt
- Low-fat or fat-free milk
- Greek yogurt
- Almond milk
- Soy milk

Fats and Oils:
- Olive oil
- Avocado
- Nuts (in moderation)
- Seeds (in moderation)

Snacks and Condiments:
- Hummus
- Salsa (low-sodium)
- Nut butter (almond or peanut butter)
- Popcorn (air-popped, no added salt or butter)
- Herbs & spices (for flavor without added salt)

Beverages:
- Water (drink plenty)
- Herbal tea (unsweetened)
- Green tea (unsweetened)
- Limited amounts of 100% fruit juice (in moderation)

Miscellaneous:
- Herbs and spices (to flavor dishes without adding salt)
- Garlic

- Onions
- Vinegar (balsamic, red wine)
- Canned tomatoes (no added salt)
- Low-sodium chicken or vegetable broth

CHAPTER 2. BREAKFAST RECIPES

1. Quinoa Breakfast Bowl

Preparation time: 15 mins

Cooking time: 15 mins

Servings: 2

Ingredients:

- 1 teacup cooked quinoa
- 1/2 teacup unsweetened almond milk
- 1/2 teacup cubed apple
- 1/4 tsp cinnamon
- 1/4 tsp vanilla extract

Directions:

1. Inside a saucepot, warm the almond milk, cubed apple, cinnamon, and vanilla extract.
2. Serve the cooked quinoa in bowls and pour the warm apple mixture over it.

Per serving: Calories: 232kcal; Fat: 4gm; Carbs: 45gm; Protein: 6gm; Sugar: 6gm; Sodium: 80mg; Potassium: 201mg

2. Oatmeal with Mixed Berries

Preparation time: 5 mins

Cooking time: 5 mins

Servings: 2

Ingredients:

- 1 teacup rolled oats
- 2 teacups unsweetened almond milk
- 1 teacup mixed berries (e.g., blueberries, strawberries, raspberries)
- 1 tbsp honey (optional)

Directions:

1. Inside a saucepot, blend oats and almond milk.
2. Cook in a middling temp., mixing irregularly till the oats are cooked then the mixture denses (around 5 mins).
3. Top with mixed berries then spray with honey if anticipated.

Per serving: Calories: 255kcal; Fat: 4gm; Carbs: 47gm; Protein: 6gm; Sugar: 7gm; Sodium: 108mg; Potassium: 180mg

3. Berry and Spinach Smoothie

Preparation time: 5 mins

Cooking time: 0 mins

Servings: 2

Ingredients:

- 2 teacups fresh spinach
- 1 teacup mixed berries (e.g., strawberries, blueberries)
- 1 banana
- 1 teacup unsweetened almond milk
- 1/2 teacup plain Greek yogurt

Directions:

1. Blend the entire components till smooth.

Per serving: Calories: 187kcal; Fat: 4gm; Carbs: 33gm; Protein: 7gm; Sugar: 17gm; Sodium: 108mg; Potassium: 450mg

4. Sweet Potato and Spinach Hash

Preparation time: 15 mins
Cooking time: 20 mins
Servings: 2
Ingredients:

- 2 teacups sweet potatoes, cubed
- 1 teacup fresh spinach
- 1/2 red bell pepper, cubed
- 1/4 tsp paprika
- 1/4 tsp cumin
- 1/4 tsp black pepper

Directions:

1. Inside a griddle, sauté sweet potatoes till they start to soften.
2. Include red bell pepper, paprika, cumin, and black pepper.
3. When the sweet potatoes are cooked through, include fresh spinach then cook till wilted.

Per serving: Calories: 206kcal; Fat: 1gm; Carbs: 45gm; Protein: 5gm; Sugar: 9gm; Sodium: 90mg; Potassium: 483mg

5. Veggie Breakfast Burrito

Preparation time: 15 mins
Cooking time: 10 mins
Servings: 2
Ingredients:

- 2 whole grain tortillas
- 4 large eggs, scrambled
- 1/2 teacup cubed bell peppers
- 1/2 teacup cubed tomatoes
- 1/4 teacup cubed red onion
- 1/4 tsp black pepper
- 1/4 tsp cayenne pepper (optional)

Directions:

1. Inside your non-stick griddle, sauté cubed bell peppers, tomatoes, and red onion till tender.
2. Include scrambled eggs then cook till they are set.
3. Season with black pepper and cayenne pepper if anticipated.
4. Divide your mixture between the tortillas and roll them up.

Per serving: Calories: 282kcal; Fat: 11gm; Carbs: 30gm; Protein: 17gm; Sugar: 4gm; Sodium: 270mg; Potassium: 424mg

6. Tofu Scramble

Preparation time: 10 mins
Cooking time: 10 mins
Servings: 2
Ingredients:

- 1/2 block extra-firm tofu, crumbled
- 1/2 teacup cubed bell peppers
- 1/2 teacup cubed tomatoes

- 1/4 teacup cubed red onion
- 1/4 tsp turmeric
- 1/4 tsp black salt (kala namak) for an eggy flavor
- 1/4 tsp black pepper

Directions:
1. Inside a griddle, sauté cubed bell peppers, tomatoes, and red onion till tender.
2. Include crumbled tofu, turmeric, black salt, and black pepper.
3. Cook, mixing irregularly, 'til the tofu is heated through.

Per serving: Calories: 141kcal; Fat: 5gm; Carbs: 9gm; Protein: 14gm; Sugar: 3gm; Sodium: 210mg; Potassium: 405mg

7. Blueberry and Almond Overnight Oats

Preparation time: 5 mins (plus chilling time)
Cooking time: 0 mins
Servings: 2
Ingredients:
- 1 teacup rolled oats
- 1 1/2 teacups unsweetened almond milk
- 1/2 teacup fresh or frozen blueberries
- 2 tbsps severed almonds
- 1 tbsp pure maple syrup

Directions:
1. Mix rolled oats, almond milk, blueberries, severed almonds, and maple syrup inside your container.
2. Cover and put in the fridge overnight.
3. Stir prior to serving.

Per serving: Calories: 258kcal; Fat: 7gm; Carbs: 40gm; Protein: 6gm; Sugar: 7gm; Sodium: 164mg; Potassium: 210mg

8. Peanut Butter and Banana Oatmeal

Preparation time: 5 mins
Cooking time: 5 mins
Servings: 2
Ingredients:
- 1 teacup rolled oats
- 2 teacups unsweetened almond milk
- 2 ripe bananas, mashed
- 2 tbsps natural peanut butter

Directions:
1. Inside a saucepot, blend oats and almond milk.
2. Cook in a middling temp., mixing irregularly till the oats are cooked then the mixture denses (around 5 mins).
3. Stir in mashed bananas and peanut butter.

Per serving: Calories: 284kcal; Fat: 9gm; Carbs: 46gm; Protein: 8gm; Sugar: 11gm; Sodium: 148mg; Potassium: 430mg

9. Veggie and Hummus Wrap

Preparation time: 10 mins

Cooking time: 0 mins

Servings: 2

Ingredients:

- 2 whole grain tortillas
- 1/2 teacup hummus
- 1/2 teacup cubed cucumbers
- 1/2 teacup cubed bell peppers
- 1/2 teacup baby spinach leaves

Directions:

1. Disperse hummus evenly on each tortilla.
2. Include cubed cucumbers, bell peppers, and baby spinach leaves to each tortilla.
3. Roll them up and enjoy.

Per serving: Calories: 266kcal; Fat: 11gm; Carbs: 33gm; Protein: 8gm; Sugar: 3gm; Sodium: 444mg; Potassium: 280mg

10. Raspberry and Almond Chia Pudding

Preparation time: 5 mins (plus chilling time)

Cooking time: 0 mins

Servings: 2

Ingredients:

- 1/4 teacup chia seeds
- 1 teacup unsweetened almond milk
- 1/2 teacup fresh raspberries
- 2 tbsps severed almonds
- 1 tbsp pure maple syrup

Directions:

1. Mix chia seeds, almond milk, raspberries, severed almonds, and maple syrup inside your container.
2. Put in the fridge for a few hrs or overnight till the mixture denses.
3. Serve topped with fresh raspberries.

Per serving: Calories: 192kcal; Fat: 9gm; Carbs: 23gm; Protein: 6gm; Sugar: 6gm; Sodium: 90mg; Potassium: 192mg

11. Mixed Berry Smoothie

Preparation time: 5 mins

Cooking time: 0 mins

Servings: 2

Ingredients:

- 1 teacup mixed berries (e.g., strawberries, blueberries, raspberries)
- 1 banana
- 1/2 teacup unsweetened almond milk
- 1/2 teacup plain Greek yogurt
- 1/4 tsp vanilla extract

Directions:

1. Blend the entire components till smooth.

Per serving: Calories: 154kcal; Fat: 3gm; Carbs: 28gm; Protein: 7gm; Sugar: 14gm; Sodium: 70mg; Potassium: 348mg

12. Cinnamon and Apple Oatmeal

Preparation time: 5 mins

Cooking time: 5 mins

Servings: 2

Ingredients:

- 1 teacup rolled oats
- 2 teacups unsweetened almond milk
- 1 apple, cubed
- 1/2 tsp cinnamon
- 1/4 tsp nutmeg

Directions:

1. Inside a saucepot, blend oats and almond milk.
2. Cook in a middling temp., mixing irregularly till the oats are cooked then the mixture denses (around 5 mins).
3. Stir in cubed apple, cinnamon, and nutmeg.

Per serving: Calories: 262kcal; Fat: 5gm; Carbs: 48gm; Protein: 6gm; Sugar: 13gm; Sodium: 180mg; Potassium: 277mg

13. Veggie and Quinoa Breakfast Bowl

Preparation time: 15 mins

Cooking time: 15 mins

Servings: 2

Ingredients:

- 1 teacup cooked quinoa
- 1/2 teacup cubed bell peppers
- 1/2 teacup cubed tomatoes
- 1/4 teacup cubed red onion
- 1/4 teacup fresh spinach leaves
- 1/4 tsp black pepper
- 1/4 tsp paprika

Directions:

1. Inside a griddle, sauté cubed bell peppers, tomatoes, and red onion till tender.
2. Include cooked quinoa, fresh spinach leaves, black pepper, and paprika.
3. Cook till the spinach wilts and everything is heated through.

Per serving: Calories: 211kcal; Fat: 2gm; Carbs: 42gm; Protein: 7gm; Sugar: 6gm; Sodium: 70mg; Potassium: 388mg

14. Almond and Banana Toast

Preparation time: 5 mins

Cooking time: 5 mins

Servings: 2

Ingredients:

- 2 slices whole grain bread
- 2 ripe bananas, sliced
- 2 tbsps almond butter

Directions:
1. Toast the bread till crispy.
2. Disperse almond butter evenly on each slice.
3. Top with banana slices.

Per serving: Calories: 253kcal; Fat: 10gm; Carbs: 37gm; Protein: 6gm; Sugar: 13gm; Sodium: 197mg; Potassium: 473mg

15. Tomato and Basil Omelet

Preparation time: 10 mins
Cooking time: 10 mins
Servings: 2
Ingredients:
- 4 large eggs
- 1/2 teacup cubed tomatoes
- 2 tbsps severed fresh basil
- 1/4 tsp black pepper

Directions:
1. Inside your container, whisk the eggs and black pepper.
2. Pour the egg mixture into your non-stick skillet.
3. Include cubed tomatoes and severed fresh basil.
4. Cook till the eggs are set, then fold the omelet in half.

Per serving: Calories: 176kcal; Fat: 11gm; Carbs: 5gm; Protein: 13gm; Sugar: 3gm; Sodium: 152mg; Potassium: 311mg

CHAPTER 3. SMOOTHIES AND SHAKES RECIPES

16. Berry Blast Smoothie

Preparation time: 5 mins

Cooking time: 0 mins

Servings: 2

Ingredients:

- 1 teacup mixed berries (strawberries, blueberries, raspberries)
- 1/2 banana
- 1 teacup unsweetened almond milk
- 1/2 teacup plain Greek yogurt
- 1 tbsp honey (optional)

Directions:

1. Blend the entire components inside a blender.
2. Blend till smooth.
3. Serve instantly.

Per serving: Calories: 127kcal; Fat: 3gm; Carbs: 21gm; Protein: 6gm; Sugar: 13gm; Sodium: 80mg; Potassium: 212mg

17. Green Power Smoothie

Preparation time: 5 mins

Cooking time: 0 mins

Servings: 2

Ingredients:

- 2 teacups spinach
- 1/2 cucumber
- 1/2 avocado
- 1/2 lemon (juiced)
- 1 teacup unsweetened almond milk
- 1 tbsp chia seeds

Directions:

1. Blend spinach, cucumber, avocado, lemon juice, and almond milk till smooth.
2. Stir in chia seeds then let it sit for a min to thicken.
3. Serve cold.

Per serving: Calories: 121kcal; Fat: 9gm; Carbs: 9gm; Protein: 3gm; Sugar: 1gm; Sodium: 120mg; Potassium: 321mg

18. Tropical Delight Smoothie

Preparation time: 5 mins

Cooking time: 0 mins

Servings: 2

Ingredients:

- 1/2 teacup pineapple chunks
- 1/2 teacup mango chunks
- 1/2 banana
- 1 teacup unsweetened coconut milk
- 1/2 teacup plain Greek yogurt

Directions:

1. Blend the entire components inside a blender.
2. Blend till smooth.
3. Serve chilled.

Per serving: Calories: 145kcal; Fat: 4gm; Carbs: 26gm; Protein: 6gm; Sugar: 16gm; Sodium: 50mg; Potassium: 265mg

19. Cinnamon Apple Smoothie

Preparation time: 5 mins

Cooking time: 0 mins

Servings: 2

Ingredients:

- 1 apple (skinned and cubed)
- 1/2 tsp cinnamon
- 1 teacup unsweetened almond milk
- 1/2 teacup plain Greek yogurt
- 1 tbsp honey (optional)

Directions:

1. Blend cubed apple, cinnamon, almond milk, yogurt, and honey inside a mixer.
2. Blend till smooth.
3. Serve instantly.

Per serving: Calories: 123kcal; Fat: 3gm; Carbs: 22gm; Protein: 6gm; Sugar: 15gm; Sodium: 108mg; Potassium: 240mg

20. Carrot Cake Smoothie

Preparation time: 5 mins

Cooking time: 0 mins

Servings: 2

Ingredients:

- 1 large carrot (skinned and cubed)
- 1/2 tsp ground cinnamon
- 1/4 tsp ground nutmeg
- 1 teacup unsweetened almond milk
- 1/2 teacup plain Greek yogurt
- 1 tbsp maple syrup (optional)

Directions:

1. Blend carrot, cinnamon, nutmeg, almond milk, yogurt, and maple syrup inside a mixer till smooth.
2. Serve chilled.

Per serving: Calories: 106kcal; Fat: 2gm; Carbs: 18gm; Protein: 5gm; Sugar: 10gm; Sodium: 100mg; Potassium: 292mg

21. Citrus Kale Smoothie

Preparation time: 5 mins

Cooking time: 0 mins

Servings: 2

Ingredients:

- 1 teacup kale leaves (stems removed)
- 1 orange (skinned and segmented)
- 1/2 lemon (juiced)
- 1/2 banana
- 1 teacup unsweetened almond milk

Directions:

1. Blend kale, orange segments, lemon juice, banana, and almond milk till smooth.
2. Serve instantly.

Per serving: Calories: 87kcal; Fat: 1gm; Carbs: 18gm; Protein: 2gm; Sugar: 9gm; Sodium: 110mg; Potassium: 335mg

22. Pomegranate Blueberry Shake

Preparation time: 5 mins
Cooking time: 0 mins
Servings: 2
Ingredients:

- 1/2 teacup pomegranate seeds
- 1/2 teacup blueberries
- 1/2 teacup unsweetened pomegranate juice
- 1/2 teacup plain Greek yogurt
- 1 tbsp honey (optional)

Directions:

1. Blend pomegranate seeds, blueberries, pomegranate juice, yogurt, and honey inside a mixer till smooth.
2. Serve cold.

Per serving: Calories: 128kcal; Fat: 1gm; Carbs: 27gm; Protein: 5gm; Sugar: 21gm; Sodium: 60mg; Potassium: 257mg

23. Cherry Almond Smoothie

Preparation time: 5 mins
Cooking time: 0 mins
Servings: 2
Ingredients:

- 1 teacup frozen cherries
- 1/4 teacup unsalted almonds
- 1 teacup unsweetened almond milk
- 1/2 tsp almond extract
- 1/2 tsp vanilla extract

Directions:

1. Blend frozen cherries, unsalted almonds, almond milk, almond extract, and vanilla extract till smooth.
2. Serve chilled.

Per serving: Calories: 154kcal; Fat: 8gm; Carbs: 18gm; Protein: 4gm; Sugar: 9gm; Sodium: 100mg; Potassium: 221mg

24. Avocado Kale Smoothie

Preparation time: 5 mins
Cooking time: 0 mins
Servings: 2
Ingredients:

- 1/2 avocado
- 1 teacup kale leaves (stems removed)
- 1/2 cucumber
- 1/2 lemon (juiced)
- 1 teacup unsweetened coconut water

Directions:

1. Blend avocado, kale, cucumber, lemon juice, and coconut water till smooth.
2. Serve over ice.

Per serving: Calories: 126kcal; Fat: 7gm; Carbs: 13gm; Protein: 3gm; Sugar: 6gm; Sodium: 140mg; Potassium: 427mg

25. Mango Spinach Smoothie

Preparation time: 5 mins

Cooking time: 0 mins

Servings: 2

Ingredients:

- 1 teacup mango chunks
- 1 teacup spinach
- 1/2 banana
- 1 teacup unsweetened coconut water

Directions:

1. Blend mango chunks, spinach, banana, and coconut water till smooth.
2. Serve cold.

Per serving: Calories: 108kcal; Fat: 1gm; Carbs: 25gm; Protein: 2gm; Sugar: 17gm; Sodium: 170mg; Potassium: 328mg

26. Raspberry Oatmeal Smoothie

Preparation time: 5 mins

Cooking time: 0 mins

Servings: 2

Ingredients:

- 1/2 teacup frozen raspberries
- 1/2 teacup rolled oats
- 1 teacup unsweetened almond milk
- 1/2 tsp vanilla extract

Directions:

1. Blend frozen raspberries, rolled oats, almond milk, and vanilla extract till smooth.
2. Serve cold.

Per serving: Calories: 151kcal; Fat: 4gm; Carbs: 25gm; Protein: 4gm; Sugar: 4gm; Sodium: 161mg; Potassium: 190mg

27. Peach Almond Smoothie

Preparation time: 5 mins

Cooking time: 0 mins

Servings: 2

Ingredients:

- 1 teacup frozen peach slices
- 1/4 teacup unsalted almonds
- 1 teacup unsweetened almond milk
- 1/2 tsp almond extract

Directions:

1. Blend frozen peach slices, unsalted almonds, almond milk, and almond extract till smooth.
2. Serve chilled.

Per serving: Calories: 127kcal; Fat: 7gm; Carbs: 13gm; Protein: 4gm; Sugar: 8gm; Sodium: 90mg; Potassium: 283mg

28. Spinach and Pineapple Smoothie

Preparation time: 5 mins

Cooking time: 0 mins

Servings: 2

Ingredients:

- 1 teacup spinach
- 1 teacup cubed pineapple
- 1/2 banana
- 1 teacup unsweetened coconut water

Directions:

1. Blend spinach, cubed pineapple, banana, and coconut water till smooth.
2. Serve cold.

Per serving: Calories: 84kcal; Fat: 0g; Carbs: 20g; Protein: 1gm; Sugar: 14gm; Sodium: 140mg; Potassium: 341mg

29. Blueberry Chia Seed Shake

Preparation time: 5 mins

Cooking time: 0 mins

Servings: 2

Ingredients:

- 1 teacup blueberries
- 1 tbsp chia seeds
- 1 teacup unsweetened almond milk
- 1/2 tsp vanilla extract

Directions:

1. Blend blueberries, chia seeds, almond milk, and vanilla extract till smooth.
2. Let it sit for a few mins to thicken.
3. Serve cold.

Per serving: Calories: 96kcal; Fat: 3gm; Carbs: 16gm; Protein: 2gm; Sugar: 7gm; Sodium: 110mg; Potassium: 208mg

30. Banana Kiwi Smoothie

Preparation time: 5 mins

Cooking time: 0 mins

Servings: 2

Ingredients:

- 2 ripe bananas
- 2 kiwis (skinned and cubed)
- 1 teacup unsweetened almond milk
- 1/2 tsp honey (optional)

Directions:

1. Blend ripe bananas, cubed kiwis, almond milk, and honey (if using) till smooth.
2. Serve instantly.

Per serving: Calories: 143kcal; Fat: 2gm; Carbs: 34gm; Protein: 2gm; Sugar: 19gm; Sodium: 90mg; Potassium: 452mg

CHAPTER 4. SNACKS RECIPES

31. Hummus and Veggie Sticks

Preparation time: 10 mins

Cooking time: 0 mins

Servings: 2

Ingredients:

- 1 teacup canned chickpeas, that is drained and washed
- 2 pieces garlic
- 2 tbsps lemon juice
- 1/4 tsp cumin
- Assorted fresh vegetable sticks (carrots, cucumber, bell peppers)

Directions:

1. Blend chickpeas, garlic, lemon juice, and cumin inside a mixer. Blend till smooth.
2. Serve with vegetable sticks.

Per serving: Calories: 125kcal; Fat: 2gm; Carbs: 22gm; Protein: 6gm; Sugar: 3gm; Sodium: 10mg; Potassium: 255mg

32. Edamame with Lemon and Sea Salt

Preparation time: 5 mins

Cooking time: 5 mins

Servings: 2

Ingredients:

- 2 teacups frozen edamame
- Zest and juice of 1 lemon
- Sea salt as required

Directions:

1. Cook edamame according to package instructions.
2. Toss with lemon zest, lemon juice, and a tweak of sea salt.

Per serving: Calories: 108kcal; Fat: 3gm; Carbs: 9gm; Protein: 8gm; Sugar: 2gm; Sodium: 5mg; Potassium: 223mg

33. Avocado and Salsa Dip

Preparation time: 5 mins

Cooking time: 0 mins

Servings: 2

Ingredients:

- 1 ripe avocado, mashed
- 1/2 teacup fresh salsa
- Sliced cucumber for dipping

Directions:

1. Mix mashed avocado and salsa inside your container.
2. Serve with cucumber slices.

Per serving: Calories: 144kcal; Fat: 10gm; Carbs: 10gm; Protein: 2gm; Sugar: 3gm; Sodium: 321mg; Potassium: 523mg

34. Grilled Vegetable Salad

Preparation time: 15 mins

Cooking time: 10 mins

Servings: 2

Ingredients:

- 2 teacups mixed grilled vegetables (e.g., bell peppers, zucchini, asparagus)
- 1/4 teacup red onion, finely cut
- 2 tbsps balsamic vinegar
- 1 tbsp olive oil
- 1/2 tsp dried thyme
- Salt and pepper as required
- Fresh basil leaves for garnish (optional)

Directions:

1. Grill the vegetables till tender then slightly charred.
2. Inside your huge container, blend grilled vegetables and red onion.
3. Inside your small container, whisk collectively balsamic vinegar, olive oil, dried thyme, salt, and pepper.
4. Transfer the dressing over the salad then toss to coat.
5. Garnish with fresh basil leaves, if anticipated.

Per serving: Calories: 151kcal; Fat: 7gm; Carbs: 20gm; Protein: 4gm; Sugar: 9gm; Sodium: 45mg; Potassium: 485mg

35. Cherry Tomatoes with Balsamic Glaze

Preparation time: 5 mins

Cooking time: 0 mins

Servings: 2

Ingredients:

- 1 teacup cherry tomatoes
- 1 tbsp balsamic glaze

Directions:

1. Arrange cherry tomatoes on a plate.
2. Spray with balsamic glaze.

Per serving: Calories: 255kcal; Fat: 0gm; Carbs: 6gm; Protein: 1gm; Sugar: 3gm; Sodium: 0mg; Potassium: 205mg

36. Spinach and Tomato Frittata

Preparation time: 10 mins

Cooking time: 15 mins

Servings: 2

Ingredients:

- 4 large eggs
- 1 teacup fresh spinach
- 1 teacup cubed tomatoes
- 1/4 tsp black pepper
- 1/4 tsp garlic powder

Directions:

1. Warm up the oven to 350 deg.F.

2. In an oven-safe skillet, sauté fresh spinach and cubed tomatoes till wilted.
3. Inside your container, whisk the eggs, black pepper, and garlic powder.
4. Place the egg mixture over the vegetables in the skillet.
5. Bake in to your warmed up oven for around 15 mins or till the frittata is set.

Per serving: Calories: 197kcal; Fat: 10gm; Carbs: 10gm; Protein: 14gm; Sugar: 4gm; Sodium: 150mg; Potassium: 461mg

37. Hard-Boiled Eggs with Mustard

Preparation time: 10 mins
Cooking time: 12 mins
Servings: 2
Ingredients:

- 2 large eggs
- 2 tsps Dijon mustard

Directions:

1. Place eggs in your saucepan and cover with water. Raise to a boil, then decrease temp. then simmer for 10-12 mins.
2. Peel eggs and cut in half. Serve with mustard for dipping.

Per serving: Calories: 88kcal; Fat: 5gm; Carbs: 1gm; Protein: 6gm; Sugar: 0gm; Sodium: 130mg; Potassium: 70mg

38. Bell Pepper and Guacamole Bites

Preparation time: 10 mins
Cooking time: 0 mins
Servings: 2
Ingredients:

- 1 bell pepper, sliced into rings
- 1/2 teacup homemade guacamole (avocado, tomato, onion, cilantro, lime juice)

Directions:

1. Fill each bell pepper ring with a spoonful of guacamole.

Per serving: Calories: 156kcal; Fat: 12gm; Carbs: 10gm; Protein: 2gm; Sugar: 3gm; Sodium: 15mg; Potassium: 407mg

39. Crispy Baked Zucchini Chips

Preparation time: 10 mins
Cooking time: 20 mins
Servings: 2
Ingredients:

- 2 small zucchinis, sliced into thin rounds
- 1 tbsp olive oil
- 1/2 tsp garlic powder

- 1/2 tsp paprika

Directions:

1. Warm up the oven to 425 deg.F.
2. Toss zucchini slices with olive oil, garlic powder, and paprika.
3. Disperse on your baking sheet then bake for 20 mins, turning once.

Per serving: Calories: 86kcal; Fat: 6gm; Carbs: 5gm; Protein: 2gm; Sugar: 2gm; Sodium: 10mg; Potassium: 306mg

40. Mango and Coconut Chia Pudding

Preparation time: 5 mins (plus chilling time)
Cooking time: 0 mins
Servings: 2
Ingredients:

- 1/4 teacup chia seeds
- 1 teacup unsweetened coconut milk
- 1/2 teacup cubed mango
- 2 tbsps shredded coconut
- 1 tbsp pure maple syrup

Directions:

1. Mix chia seeds, coconut milk, cubed mango, shredded coconut, and maple syrup inside your container.
2. Put in the fridge for a few hrs or overnight till the mixture denses.
3. Serve topped with additional cubed mango and shredded coconut.

Per serving: Calories: 231kcal; Fat: 14gm; Carbs: 26gm; Protein: 5gm; Sugar: 15gm; Sodium: 80mg; Potassium: 221mg

41. Tuna and Cucumber Boats

Preparation time: 10 mins
Cooking time: 0 mins
Servings: 2
Ingredients:

- 1 tin (5 oz) tuna in water, drained
- 1/4 teacup cubed cucumber
- 1 tbsp lemon juice
- Freshly ground black pepper as required

Directions:

1. Mix tuna, cucumber, lemon juice, and black pepper inside your container.
2. Spoon the mixture into cucumber boats (cucumber halves).

Per serving: Calories: 76kcal; Fat: 0gm; Carbs: 1gm; Protein: 16gm; Sugar: 0gm; Sodium: 131mg; Potassium: 178mg

42. Cauliflower Popcorn

Preparation time: 10 mins
Cooking time: 20 mins
Servings: 2
Ingredients:

- 2 teacups cauliflower florets
- 1 tbsp olive oil
- 1/2 tsp smoked paprika

- 1/2 tsp garlic powder

Directions:
1. Warm up the oven to 425 deg.F.
2. Toss cauliflower florets with olive oil, smoked paprika, and garlic powder.
3. Disperse on your baking sheet then bake for 20 mins, till crispy.

Per serving: Calories: 66kcal; Fat: 4gm; Carbs: 6gm; Protein: 2gm; Sugar: 2gm; Sodium: 30mg; Potassium: 280mg

43. Watermelon and Mint Skewers

Preparation time: 10 mins
Cooking time: 0 mins
Servings: 2
Ingredients:
- 1 teacup watermelon cubes
- Fresh mint leaves

Directions:
1. Thread watermelon cubes and mint leaves onto skewers.

Per serving: Calories: 22kcal; Fat: 0gm; Carbs: 5gm; Protein: 0gm; Sugar: 4gm; Sodium: 0mg; Potassium: 90mg

44. Quinoa Salad

Preparation time: 15 mins
Cooking time: 0 mins
Servings: 2
Ingredients:
- 1/2 teacup cooked quinoa
- 1/2 teacup cubed cucumber
- 1/2 teacup cubed tomatoes
- 2 tbsps fresh lemon juice
- Fresh parsley for garnish

Directions:
1. Blend quinoa, cucumber, and tomatoes inside your container.
2. Spray with fresh lemon juice then garnish with fresh parsley.

Per serving: Calories: 97kcal; Fat: 1gm; Carbs: 19gm; Protein: 3gm; Sugar: 2gm; Sodium: 10mg; Potassium: 266mg

45. Chia Pudding with Berries

Preparation time: 5 mins
Cooking time: 0 mins
Servings: 2
Ingredients:
- 1/4 teacup chia seeds
- 1 teacup unsweetened almond milk
- 1/2 teacup mixed berries (strawberries, blueberries, raspberries)

Directions:
1. Mix chia seeds and almond milk inside your container. Stir well.
2. Put in the fridge for almost 4 hrs (or overnight) till it denses.
3. Serve with mixed berries on top.

Per serving: Calories: 101kcal; Fat: 5gm; Carbs: 11gm; Protein: 3gm; Sugar: 2gm; Sodium: 60mg; Potassium: 132mg

CHAPTER 5. SAUCE AND SPICE-BASED SEASONINGS RECIPES TO NOT MISS THE SALT ON FOODS

46. Lemon Herb Sauce

Preparation time: 5 mins

Cooking time: 5 mins

Servings: 2

Ingredients:

- 1 lemon (juice and zest)
- 1 tsp dried oregano
- 1 tsp dried thyme
- 1 piece garlic, crushed

Directions:

1. Mix lemon juice, zest, oregano, thyme, and crushed garlic inside your container.
2. Simmer in your saucepan for 5 mins.

Per serving: Calories: 16kcal; Fat: 0gm; Carbs: 3gm; Protein: 0gm; Sugar: 0gm; Sodium: 0mg; Potassium: 20mg

47. Garlic and Herb Seasoning

Preparation time: 5 mins

Cooking time: 0 mins

Servings: 2

Ingredients:

- 2 pieces garlic, crushed
- 1 tsp dried basil
- 1 tsp dried rosemary
- 1 tsp dried parsley

Directions:

1. Mix crushed garlic, basil, rosemary, and parsley.
2. Store in an airtight container.

Per serving: Calories: 55kcal; Fat: 0gm; Carbs: 1gm; Protein: 0gm; Sugar: 0gm; Sodium: 0mg; Potassium: 10mg

48. Ginger Sesame Dressing

Preparation time: 10 mins

Cooking time: 0 mins

Servings: 2

Ingredients:

- 1 tbsp grated ginger
- 1 tbsp low-sodium soy sauce
- 1 tbsp rice vinegar
- 1 tsp sesame oil

Directions:

1. Mix grated ginger, soy sauce, rice vinegar, and sesame oil.
2. Shake well prior to serving.

Per serving: Calories: 23kcal; Fat: 2gm; Carbs: 1gm; Protein: 0gm; Sugar: 0gm; Sodium: 141mg; Potassium: 10mg

49. Chili-Lime Seasoning

Preparation time: 5 mins

Cooking time: 0 mins

Servings: 2

Ingredients:

- 1 tsp chili powder
- 1 tsp paprika
- Zest of 1 lime
- 1/2 tsp cayenne pepper (as required)

Directions:

1. Mix chili powder, paprika, lime zest, and cayenne pepper.
2. Use as a seasoning for your grilled fish or vegetables.

Per serving: Calories: 58kcal; Fat: 0gm; Carbs: 1gm; Protein: 0gm; Sugar: 0gm; Sodium: 0mg; Potassium: 10mg

50. Balsamic Dijon Vinaigrette

Preparation time: 5 mins
Cooking time: 0 mins
Servings: 2

Ingredients:

- 2 tbsps balsamic vinegar
- 1 tbsp Dijon mustard
- 1/2 tsp honey (optional)

Directions:

1. Whisk together balsamic vinegar, Dijon mustard, and honey.
2. Spray over salads or roasted vegetables.

Per serving: Calories: 27kcal; Fat: 0gm; Carbs: 5gm; Protein: 0gm; Sugar: 3gm; Sodium: 105mg; Potassium: 0mg

51. Turmeric and Cumin Seasoning

Preparation time: 5 mins
Cooking time: 0 mins
Servings: 2

Ingredients:

- 1 tsp ground turmeric
- 1 tsp ground cumin
- 1/2 tsp ground coriander
- 1/4 tsp black pepper

Directions:

1. Mix ground turmeric, cumin, coriander, and black pepper.
2. Use as a seasoning for roasted vegetables or lean protein.

Per serving: Calories: 57kcal; Fat: 0gm; Carbs: 1gm; Protein: 0gm; Sugar: 0gm; Sodium: 0mg; Potassium: 10mg

52. Lemon Pepper Seasoning

Preparation time: 5 mins
Cooking time: 0 mins
Servings: 2

Ingredients:

- Zest of 2 lemons
- 1 tsp black pepper
- 1/2 tsp garlic powder

Directions:

1. Blend black pepper, lemon zest, and garlic powder.

2. Use as a seasoning for your grilled or roasted vegetables.

Per serving: Calories: 53kcal; Fat: 0gm; Carbs: 1gm; Protein: 0gm; Sugar: 0gm; Sodium: 0mg; Potassium: 0mg

53. Rosemary Dijon Marinade

Preparation time: 5 mins

Cooking time: 0 mins

Servings: 2

Ingredients:

- 2 tbsps Dijon mustard
- 1 tsp dried rosemary
- 1 piece garlic, crushed

Directions:

1. Mix Dijon mustard, dried rosemary, and crushed garlic.
2. Use as a marinade for chicken or pork.

Per serving: Calories: 35kcal; Fat: 1gm; Carbs: 6gm; Protein: 1gm; Sugar: 1gm; Sodium: 287mg; Potassium: 0mg

54. Lemon Basil Pesto

Preparation time: 10 mins

Cooking time: 0 mins

Servings: 2

Ingredients:

- 1 teacup fresh basil leaves
- Juice of 1 lemon
- 1 piece garlic
- 2 tbsps pine nuts

Directions:

1. Blend basil leaves, lemon juice, garlic, and pine nuts in a food processor till smooth.
2. Use as a sauce for whole-grain pasta or grilled vegetables.

Per serving: Calories: 86kcal; Fat: 7gm; Carbs: 4gm; Protein: 2gm; Sugar: 0gm; Sodium: 0mg; Potassium: 90mg

55. Spicy Tomato Salsa

Preparation time: 10 mins

Cooking time: 0 mins

Servings: 2

Ingredients:

- 2 tomatoes, cubed
- 1/2 onion, finely severed
- 1/2 jalapeño pepper, seeded and crushed
- 2 tbsps fresh cilantro, severed

Directions:

1. Blend cubed tomatoes, severed onion, crushed jalapeño pepper, and severed cilantro.
2. Serve as a salsa for grilled chicken or as a dip for whole-grain tortilla chips.

Per serving: Calories: 22kcal; Fat: 0gm; Carbs: 5gm; Protein: 1gm; Sugar: 2gm; Sodium: 5mg; Potassium: 223mg

56. Cumin-Lime Dressing

Preparation time: 5 mins

Cooking time: 0 mins

Servings: 2

Ingredients:

- Juice of 2 limes
- 1/2 tsp ground cumin
- 1/4 tsp ground coriander

Directions:

1. Whisk together lime juice, ground cumin, and ground coriander.
2. Spray over mixed greens or roasted vegetables.

Per serving: Calories: 13kcal; Fat: 0gm; Carbs: 3gm; Protein: 0gm; Sugar: 0gm; Sodium: 0mg; Potassium: 10mg

57. Basil Tomato Sauce

Preparation time: 15 mins

Cooking time: 15 mins

Servings: 2

Ingredients:

- 2 tomatoes, cubed
- 1/2 teacup fresh basil leaves, severed
- 1 piece garlic, crushed

Directions:

1. Inside a saucepot, blend cubed tomatoes, severed basil leaves, and crushed garlic.
2. Simmer for 15 mins, mixing irregularly.

Per serving: Calories: 38kcal; Fat: 0gm; Carbs: 7gm; Protein: 1gm; Sugar: 3gm; Sodium: 10mg; Potassium: 365mg

58. Lemon Dill Dressing

Preparation time: 5 mins

Cooking time: 0 mins

Servings: 2

Ingredients:

- Juice of 2 lemons
- 1 tsp dried dill
- 1/2 tsp black pepper

Directions:

1. Whisk together lemon juice, dried dill, and black pepper.
2. Spray over steamed vegetables or use as a salad dressing.

Per serving: Calories: 19kcal; Fat: 0gm; Carbs: 3gm; Protein: 0gm; Sugar: 1gm; Sodium: 0mg; Potassium: 20mg

59. Mediterranean Herb Blend

Preparation time: 5 mins

Cooking time: 0 mins

Servings: 2

Ingredients:

- 1 tsp dried oregano
- 1 tsp dried basil
- 1/2 tsp dried thyme
- 1/2 tsp dried marjoram

Directions:

1. Mix dried oregano, dried basil, dried thyme, and dried marjoram.
2. Use as a seasoning for your grilled or roasted vegetables.

Per serving: Calories: 57kcal; Fat: 0gm; Carbs: 1gm; Protein: 0gm; Sugar: 0gm; Sodium: 0mg; Potassium: 10mg

60. Sesame Ginger Sauce

Preparation time: 10 mins
Cooking time: 5 mins
Servings: 2

Ingredients:

- 1 tbsp low-sodium soy sauce
- 1 tbsp rice vinegar
- 1 tsp sesame oil
- 1/2 tsp grated ginger

Directions:

1. Inside a saucepot, blend soy sauce, rice vinegar, sesame oil, and grated ginger.
2. Simmer for 5 mins, then let cool.

Per serving: Calories: 24kcal; Fat: 2gm; Carbs: 1gm; Protein: 0gm; Sugar: 0gm; Sodium: 140mg; Potassium: 0mg

CHAPTER 6. SALADS RECIPES

61. Lemon Herb Quinoa Salad

Preparation time: 15 mins
Cooking time: 15 mins
Servings: 2
Ingredients:

- 1/2 teacup quinoa, cooked and cooled
- 1 teacup cucumber, cubed
- 1 teacup cherry tomatoes, halved
- 1/4 teacup fresh parsley, severed
- 2 tbsps lemon juice
- 1 tbsp olive oil
- 1/2 tsp dried oregano
- Salt and pepper as required

Directions:

1. Inside your huge container, blend quinoa, cucumber, cherry tomatoes, and parsley.
2. Inside your small container, whisk collectively lemon juice, olive oil, oregano, salt, and pepper.
3. Transfer the dressing over the salad then toss to blend.
4. Serve chilled.

Per serving: Calories: 256kcal; Fat: 8gm; Carbs: 38gm; Protein: 6gm; Sugar: 2gm; Sodium: 10mg; Potassium: 335mg

62. Mediterranean Lentil Salad

Preparation time: 20 mins
Cooking time: 20 mins
Servings: 2
Ingredients:

- 1/2 teacup dried green lentils, cooked and cooled
- 1 teacup cucumber, cubed
- 1/2 teacup red bell pepper, cubed
- 1/4 teacup red onion, finely severed
- 2 tbsps fresh lemon juice
- 1 tbsp olive oil
- 1/2 tsp dried thyme
- Salt and pepper as required

Directions:

1. Inside your huge container, blend cooked lentils, cucumber, red bell pepper, and red onion.
2. Inside your small container, whisk collectively lemon juice, olive oil, dried thyme, salt, and pepper.
3. Transfer the dressing over the salad then toss to mix.
4. Put in the fridge for 1 hour prior to serving.

Per serving: Calories: 281kcal; Fat: 6gm; Carbs: 44gm; Protein: 13gm; Sugar: 4gm; Sodium: 15mg; Potassium: 463mg

63. Tuna and White Bean Salad

Preparation time: 10 mins
Cooking time: 0 mins
Servings: 2
Ingredients:

- 1 tin (5 oz.) tuna in water, drained
- 1 tin (15 oz.) white beans, that is drained and washed
- 1 teacup cherry tomatoes, halved
- 1/4 teacup red onion, finely severed
- 2 tbsps red wine vinegar
- 1 tbsp olive oil
- 1/2 tsp dried rosemary
- Salt and pepper as required

Directions:

1. Inside your huge container, blend tuna, white beans, cherry tomatoes, and red onion.
2. Inside your small container, whisk collectively red wine vinegar, olive oil, dried rosemary, salt, and pepper.
3. Transfer the dressing over the salad then toss to coat.
4. Serve chilled.

Per serving: Calories: 346kcal; Fat: 9gm; Carbs: 42gm; Protein: 26gm; Sugar: 5gm; Sodium: 40mg; Potassium: 533mg

64. Asian-Inspired Edamame Salad

Preparation time: 15 mins
Cooking time: 5 mins
Servings: 2
Ingredients:

- 1 teacup shelled edamame, cooked and cooled
- 1 teacup red cabbage, finely cut
- 1/2 teacup carrot, shredded
- 2 tbsps rice vinegar
- 1 tbsp low-sodium soy sauce
- 1/2 tsp sesame oil
- 1/2 tsp honey or agave nectar (for sweetness, optional)
- Sesame seeds for garnish (optional)

Directions:

1. Inside your huge container, blend edamame, red cabbage, and shredded carrot.
2. Inside your small container, whisk collectively rice vinegar, soy sauce, sesame oil, and honey (if using).
3. Transfer the dressing over the salad then toss to blend.
4. Garnish with sesame seeds, if anticipated.

Per serving: Calories: 187kcal; Fat: 6gm; Carbs: 21gm; Protein: 10gm; Sugar: 7gm; Sodium: 250mg; Potassium: 470mg

65. Spinach and Strawberry Salad

Preparation time: 10 mins
Cooking time: 0 mins
Servings: 2
Ingredients:

- 2 teacups fresh spinach leaves
- 1 teacup strawberries, sliced
- 1/4 teacup red onion, finely cut
- 2 tbsps balsamic vinegar
- 1 tbsp olive oil
- 1/2 tsp Dijon mustard
- Salt and pepper as required

Directions:

1. Inside your huge container, blend spinach, strawberries, and red onion.
2. Inside your small container, whisk collectively balsamic vinegar, olive oil, Dijon mustard, salt, and pepper.
3. Transfer the dressing over the salad then toss to coat.
4. Serve instantly.

Per serving: Calories: 126kcal; Fat: 7gm; Carbs: 15gm; Protein: 2gm; Sugar: 7gm; Sodium: 65mg; Potassium: 341mg

66. Black Bean and Corn Salad

Preparation time: 15 mins
Cooking time: 0 mins
Servings: 2
Ingredients:

- 1 tin (15 oz.) black beans, that is drained and washed
- 1/2 teacup red bell pepper, cubed
- 1/4 teacup red onion, finely severed
- 1 teacup corn kernels (frozen, fresh, or canned)
- 2 tbsps lime juice
- 1 tbsp olive oil
- 1/2 tsp ground cumin
- Salt and pepper as required
- Fresh cilantro leaves for garnish (optional)

Directions:

1. Inside your huge container, blend black beans, corn, red bell pepper, and red onion.
2. Inside your small container, whisk collectively lime juice, olive oil, ground cumin, salt, and pepper.
3. Transfer the dressing over the salad then toss to coat.
4. Garnish with fresh cilantro leaves, if anticipated.

Per serving: Calories: 296kcal; Fat: 8gm; Carbs: 46gm; Protein: 11gm; Sugar: 5gm; Sodium: 340mg; Potassium: 541mg

67. Spinach and Chickpea Salad with Lemon Tahini Dressing

Preparation time: 15 mins
Cooking time: 0 mins
Servings: 2
Ingredients:

- 2 teacups fresh spinach leaves
- 1 tin (15 oz.) chickpeas, that is drained and washed
- 1/4 teacup red bell pepper, cubed
- 2 tbsps tahini
- 2 tbsps lemon juice
- 1 piece garlic, crushed
- 1/2 tsp ground cumin
- Salt and pepper as required

Directions:

1. Inside your huge container, blend fresh spinach, chickpeas, and red bell pepper.
2. Inside your small container, whisk collectively tahini, lemon juice, salt, crushed garlic, ground cumin, and pepper.
3. Transfer the dressing over the salad then toss to mix.
4. Serve instantly.

Per serving: Calories: 285kcal; Fat: 11gm; Carbs: 35gm; Protein: 12gm; Sugar: 5gm; Sodium: 190mg; Potassium: 563mg

68. Caprese Salad with Balsamic Glaze

Preparation time: 10 mins
Cooking time: 0 mins
Servings: 2
Ingredients:

- 2 large tomatoes, sliced
- 1 teacup fresh mozzarella balls (small)
- 1/4 teacup fresh basil leaves
- 2 tbsps balsamic glaze
- 1 tbsp olive oil
- Salt and pepper as required

Directions:

1. Arrange tomato slices, mozzarella balls, and fresh basil on a plate.
2. Spray with balsamic glaze and olive oil.
3. Season with salt and pepper.
4. Serve instantly.

Per serving: Calories: 327kcal; Fat: 24gm; Carbs: 12gm; Protein: 15gm; Sugar: 8gm; Sodium: 313mg; Potassium: 465mg

69. Spinach and Avocado Salad with Cilantro Lime Dressing

Preparation time: 15 mins
Cooking time: 0 mins
Servings: 2
Ingredients:

- 2 teacups fresh spinach leaves
- 1 avocado, sliced
- 1/4 teacup red onion, finely cut
- 2 tbsps fresh lime juice
- 1 tbsp olive oil
- 2 tbsps fresh cilantro, severed
- Salt and pepper as required

Directions:
1. Inside your huge container, blend fresh spinach, avocado slices, and red onion.
2. Inside your small container, whisk collectively lime juice, olive oil, fresh cilantro, salt, and pepper.
3. Transfer the dressing over the salad then toss to mix.
4. Serve instantly.

Per serving: Calories: 251kcal; Fat: 21gm; Carbs: 15gm; Protein: 3gm; Sugar: 2gm; Sodium: 25mg; Potassium: 520mg

70. Mediterranean Chickpea Salad

Preparation time: 15 mins
Cooking time: 0 mins
Servings: 2
Ingredients:
- 1 tin (15 oz.) chickpeas, that is drained and washed

- 1/2 teacup cucumber, cubed
- 1/2 teacup cherry tomatoes, halved
- 1/4 teacup red onion, finely severed
- 2 tbsps fresh lemon juice
- 1 tbsp olive oil
- 1/2 tsp dried oregano
- Salt and pepper as required

Directions:
1. Inside your huge container, blend chickpeas, cucumber, cherry tomatoes, and red onion.
2. Inside your small container, whisk collectively fresh lemon juice, salt, olive oil, dried oregano, and pepper.
3. Transfer the dressing over the salad then toss to coat.
4. Serve chilled.

Per serving: Calories: 276kcal; Fat: 8gm; Carbs: 41gm; Protein: 11gm; Sugar: 8gm; Sodium: 40mg; Potassium: 517mg

71. Roasted Sweet Potato and Kale Salad

Preparation time: 15 mins
Cooking time: 25 mins
Servings: 2
Ingredients:
- 1 large sweet potato, skinned and cubed

- 2 teacups kale leaves, stemmed and torn into pieces
- 1/4 teacup red onion, finely cut
- 2 tbsps balsamic vinegar
- 1 tbsp olive oil
- 1/2 tsp dried rosemary
- Salt and pepper as required

Directions:
1. Warm up the oven to 400 deg.F.
2. Toss sweet potato cubes with olive oil, dried rosemary, salt, and pepper.
3. Roast sweet potatoes for 25 mins or 'til tender and slightly caramelized.
4. Inside your huge container, blend roasted sweet potatoes, kale, and red onion.
5. Inside your small container, whisk collectively balsamic vinegar and a little olive oil.
6. Transfer the dressing over the salad then toss to mix.
7. Serve warm.

Per serving: Calories: 264kcal; Fat: 7gm; Carbs: 45gm; Protein: 6gm; Sugar: 9gm; Sodium: 80mg; Potassium: 432mg

72. Waldorf Salad with Greek Yogurt Dressing

Preparation time: 15 mins
Cooking time: 0 mins
Servings: 2

Ingredients:
- 2 teacups mixed greens (e.g., spinach, lettuce)
- 1 apple, cubed
- 1/2 teacup celery, cubed
- 1/4 teacup walnuts, severed
- 2 tbsps Greek yogurt
- 1 tbsp honey
- 1/2 tsp lemon juice
- 1/4 tsp cinnamon
- Salt as required

Directions:
1. Inside your huge container, blend mixed greens, cubed apple, celery, and severed walnuts.
2. Inside your small container, whisk collectively Greek yogurt, honey, lemon juice, cinnamon, and a tweak of salt.
3. Transfer the dressing over the salad then toss to coat.
4. Serve instantly.

Per serving: Calories: 292kcal; Fat: 12gm; Carbs: 43gm; Protein: 5gm; Sugar: 30gm; Sodium: 70mg; Potassium: 412mg

73. Roasted Beet and Orange Salad

Preparation time: 15 mins
Cooking time: 45 mins
Servings: 2

Ingredients:

- 2 medium beets, roasted, skinned, and sliced
- 2 oranges, skinned and segmented
- 1/4 teacup red onion, finely cut
- 2 tbsps balsamic vinegar
- 1 tbsp olive oil
- 1/2 tsp honey or agave nectar (for sweetness, optional)
- Fresh mint leaves for garnish (optional)

Directions:

1. Roast the beets in your oven at 400 deg.F for 45 mins or till tender. Let them cool, then peel and slice.
2. Inside your huge container, blend roasted beets, orange segments, and red onion.
3. Inside your small container, whisk collectively balsamic vinegar, olive oil, and honey (if using).
4. Transfer the dressing over the salad then toss to mix.
5. Garnish with fresh mint leaves, if anticipated.

Per serving: Calories: 229kcal; Fat: 7gm; Carbs: 39gm; Protein: 3gm; Sugar: 26gm; Sodium: 70mg; Potassium: 623mg

74. Spinach and Pear Salad with Dijon Vinaigrette

Preparation time: 15 mins
Cooking time: 0 mins
Servings: 2
Ingredients:

- 2 teacups fresh spinach leaves
- 1 pear, sliced
- 1/4 teacup pecans, severed
- 2 tbsps white wine vinegar
- 1 tbsp olive oil
- 1 tsp Dijon mustard
- Salt and pepper as required

Directions:

1. Inside your huge container, blend fresh spinach, pear slices, and severed pecans.
2. Inside your small container, whisk collectively white wine vinegar, salt, olive oil, Dijon mustard, and pepper.
3. Transfer the dressing over the salad then toss to coat.
4. Serve instantly.

Per serving: Calories: 253kcal; Fat: 17gm; Carbs: 23gm; Protein: 3gm; Sugar: 12gm; Sodium: 140mg; Potassium: 360mg

75. Broccoli and Chickpea Salad with Lemon Garlic Dressing

Preparation time: 15 mins

Cooking time: 5 mins

Servings: 2

Ingredients:

- 2 teacups broccoli florets, blanched and cooled
- 1 tin (15 oz.) chickpeas, that is drained and washed
- 1/4 teacup red onion, finely severed
- 2 tbsps fresh lemon juice
- 1 tbsp olive oil
- 1 piece garlic, crushed
- Salt and pepper as required

Directions:

1. Inside your huge container, blend blanched broccoli florets, chickpeas, and red onion.
2. Inside your small container, whisk collectively fresh lemon juice, salt, olive oil, crushed garlic, and pepper.
3. Transfer the dressing over the salad then toss to mix.
4. Serve chilled.

Per serving: Calories: 295kcal; Fat: 8gm; Carbs: 45gm; Protein: 13gm; Sugar: 8gm; Sodium: 280mg; Potassium: 550mg

CHAPTER 7. POULTRY RECIPES

76. Baked Herb-Crusted Turkey Brest

Preparation time: 10 mins

Cooking time: 30 mins

Servings: 2

Ingredients:

- 2 boneless turkey breast fillets
- 1 tsp dried rosemary
- 1 tsp dried thyme
- 1 tsp paprika
- 1 piece garlic, crushed
- Black pepper as required

Directions:

1. Warm up the oven to 375 deg.F.
2. Mix herbs, paprika, garlic, and black pepper.
3. Coat turkey with the herb mixture then bake till done.

Per serving: Calories: 167kcal; Fat: 2gm; Carbs: 2gm; Protein: 35gm; Sugar: 0gm; Sodium: 60mg; Potassium: 381mg

77. Citrus-Marinated Grilled Chicken

Preparation time: 20 mins

Cooking time: 15 mins

Servings: 2

Ingredients:

- 2 boneless, skinless chicken breasts
- Juice of 1 orange
- Juice of 1 lime
- 1 tsp cumin
- 1 tsp paprika
- 1 piece garlic, crushed

Directions:

1. Blend citrus juices, cumin, paprika, and garlic.
2. Marinate chicken for 1 hour.
3. Grill till cooked through.

Per serving: Calories: 178kcal; Fat: 2gm; Carbs: 6gm; Protein: 32gm; Sugar: 2gm; Sodium: 40mg; Potassium: 430mg

78. Herbed Chicken Stir-Fry

Preparation time: 15 mins

Cooking time: 15 mins

Servings: 2

Ingredients:

- 2 boneless, skinless chicken breasts, cubed
- 1 teacup broccoli florets
- 1 teacup bell peppers, sliced
- 1 teacup snap peas
- 1 tsp dried basil
- 1 tsp dried oregano
- 1 tsp low-sodium soy sauce
- 1 piece garlic, crushed

Directions:

1. Stir-fry chicken till no longer pink, then set aside.
2. Stir-fry vegetables with garlic and soy sauce.
3. Return chicken to the pan, include herbs, then cook for an extra 2 mins.

Per serving: Calories: 186kcal; Fat: 2gm; Carbs: 11gm; Protein: 32gm; Sugar: 4gm; Sodium: 120mg; Potassium: 453mg

79. Cilantro Lime Chicken Tenders

Preparation time: 15 mins
Cooking time: 15 mins
Servings: 2
Ingredients:

- 8 chicken tenders
- Juice of 2 limes
- 1/4 teacup fresh cilantro, severed
- 1 tsp ground cumin
- 1 piece garlic, crushed
- Black pepper as required

Directions:

1. Inside your container, blend lime juice, cilantro, cumin, garlic, and black pepper.
2. Marinate chicken tenders for 30 mins.
3. Grill till cooked through.

Per serving: Calories: 166kcal; Fat: 2gm; Carbs: 3gm; Protein: 30gm; Sugar: 0gm; Sodium: 40mg; Potassium: 320mg

80. Rosemary Dijon Chicken

Preparation time: 15 mins
Cooking time: 20 mins
Servings: 2
Ingredients:

- 2 boneless, skinless chicken breasts
- 2 tbsps Dijon mustard
- 1 tsp dried rosemary
- 1 piece garlic, crushed
- Black pepper as required

Directions:

1. Mix Dijon mustard, rosemary, garlic, and black pepper.
2. Coat chicken with the mixture then bake till done.

Per serving: Calories: 171kcal; Fat: 2gm; Carbs: 2gm; Protein: 36gm; Sugar: 0gm; Sodium: 180mg; Potassium: 351mg

81. Ginger Sesame Chicken Stir-Fry

Preparation time: 15 mins
Cooking time: 15 mins
Servings: 2
Ingredients:

- 2 boneless, skinless chicken breasts, sliced

- 1 teacup broccoli florets
- 1 teacup snap peas
- 1 tbsp low-sodium soy sauce
- 1 tbsp sesame oil
- 1 tsp fresh ginger, crushed
- 1 piece garlic, crushed

Directions:

1. Stir-fry chicken till cooked through, then set aside.
2. Stir-fry vegetables with garlic, ginger, soy sauce, and sesame oil.
3. Return chicken to the pan then cook for an extra 2 mins.

Per serving: Calories: 195kcal; Fat: 5gm; Carbs: 8gm; Protein: 28gm; Sugar: 2gm; Sodium: 180mg; Potassium: 458mg

82. Paprika Chicken with Roasted Vegetables

Preparation time: 15 mins

Cooking time: 30 mins

Servings: 2

Ingredients:

- 2 boneless, skinless chicken breasts
- 1 tsp smoked paprika
- 1 tsp dried thyme
- 1 piece garlic, crushed
- 1 red bell pepper, sliced
- 1 zucchini, sliced

Directions:

1. Warm up oven to 375 deg.F.
2. Mix paprika, thyme, and garlic.
3. Coat chicken with the spice mixture then bake till done.
4. Roast vegetables in the oven till tender.

Per serving: Calories: 183kcal; Fat: 2gm; Carbs: 8gm; Protein: 32gm; Sugar: 4gm; Sodium: 50mg; Potassium: 451mg

83. Honey Mustard Chicken with Steamed Asparagus

Preparation time: 10 mins

Cooking time: 20 mins

Servings: 2

Ingredients:

- 2 boneless, skinless chicken breasts
- 2 tbsps Dijon mustard
- 1 tbsp honey
- 1 piece garlic, crushed
- 1 bunch asparagus, clipped

Directions:

1. Mix Dijon mustard, honey, and garlic.
2. Coat chicken with the honey mustard mixture then bake till done.
3. Steam asparagus till tender.

Per serving: Calories: 195kcal; Fat: 2gm; Carbs: 13gm; Protein: 32gm; Sugar: 10gm; Sodium: 180mg; Potassium: 471mg

84. Tomato Basil Chicken

Preparation time: 10 mins

Cooking time: 25 mins

Servings: 2

Ingredients:

- 2 boneless, skinless chicken breasts
- 2 tomatoes, cubed
- 1/4 teacup fresh basil, severed
- 1 piece garlic, crushed
- Black pepper as required

Directions:

1. Warm up oven to 375 deg.F.
2. Put chicken in a baking dish and top with cubed tomatoes, basil, garlic, and black pepper.
3. Bake till chicken is cooked through.

Per serving: Calories: 155kcal; Fat: 2gm; Carbs: 8gm; Protein: 30gm; Sugar: 4gm; Sodium: 60mg; Potassium: 632mg

85. Curry Chicken with Cauliflower Rice

Preparation time: 15 mins

Cooking time: 20 mins

Servings: 2

Ingredients:

- 2 boneless, skinless chicken breasts, cubed
- 1 tsp curry powder
- 1/2 tsp turmeric
- 1/2 tsp cumin
- 1/2 tsp paprika
- 1/4 tsp cinnamon
- 1 piece garlic, crushed
- 1 head cauliflower, grated (for cauliflower rice)

Directions:

1. Inside a pan, sauté chicken with spices and garlic till cooked through.
2. Make cauliflower rice by grating cauliflower and microwaving for 5 mins.
3. Serve chicken over cauliflower rice.

Per serving: Calories: 181kcal; Fat: 2gm; Carbs: 9gm; Protein: 30gm; Sugar: 3gm; Sodium: 90mg; Potassium: 614mg

86. Herb-Crusted Chicken with Sautéed Spinach

Preparation time: 10 mins

Cooking time: 20 mins

Servings: 2

Ingredients:

- 2 boneless, skinless chicken breasts
- 2 tbsps fresh parsley, severed
- 1 tsp dried thyme
- 1 tsp dried basil
- 1 piece garlic, crushed
- 4 teacups fresh spinach

Directions:

1. Mix parsley, thyme, basil, and garlic.
2. Coat chicken with the herb mixture and pan-sear till done.
3. Sauté spinach till wilted.

Per serving: Calories: 167kcal; Fat: 3gm; Carbs: 6gm; Protein: 30gm; Sugar: 1gm; Sodium: 100mg; Potassium: 513mg

87. Teriyaki Chicken with Broccoli

Preparation time: 15 mins
Cooking time: 15 mins
Servings: 2
Ingredients:

- 2 boneless, skinless chicken breasts, sliced
- 1 teacup broccoli florets
- 2 tbsps low-sodium teriyaki sauce
- 1 piece garlic, crushed

Directions:

1. Stir-fry chicken till cooked through, then set aside.
2. Stir-fry broccoli with garlic and teriyaki sauce.
3. Return chicken to the pan then cook for an extra 2 mins.

Per serving: Calories: 177kcal; Fat: 2gm; Carbs: 8gm; Protein: 30gm; Sugar: 3gm; Sodium: 290mg; Potassium: 551mg

88. Almond-Crusted Chicken Tenders

Preparation time: 15 mins
Cooking time: 20 mins
Servings: 2
Ingredients:

- 8 chicken tenders
- 1/2 teacup ground almonds
- 1 tsp dried thyme
- 1/2 tsp paprika
- 1/4 tsp black pepper
- 1/4 tsp garlic powder

Directions:

1. Inside your container, mix ground almonds, thyme, paprika, black pepper, and garlic powder.
2. Coat chicken tenders with the almond mixture then bake till done.

Per serving: Calories: 206kcal; Fat: 9gm; Carbs: 5gm; Protein: 28gm; Sugar: 1gm; Sodium: 70mg; Potassium: 380mg

89. Pineapple Teriyaki Chicken

Preparation time: 15 mins
Cooking time: 15 mins
Servings: 2
Ingredients:

- 2 boneless, skinless chicken breasts, sliced
- 1 teacup pineapple chunks
- 2 tbsps low-sodium teriyaki sauce
- 1 piece garlic, crushed

Directions:

1. Stir-fry chicken till cooked through, then set aside.

2. Stir-fry pineapple with garlic and teriyaki sauce.
3. Return chicken to the pan then cook for an extra 2 mins.

Per serving: Calories: 183kcal; Fat: 2gm; Carbs: 16gm; Protein: 28gm; Sugar: 11gm; Sodium: 240mg; Potassium: 450mg

90. Spicy Cajun Chicken with Sautéed Spinach

Preparation time: 10 mins
Cooking time: 20 mins
Servings: 2
Ingredients:

- 2 boneless, skinless chicken breasts
- 1 tsp Cajun seasoning
- 1/2 tsp paprika
- 1/4 tsp cayenne pepper (as required)
- 1 piece garlic, crushed
- 4 teacups fresh spinach

Directions:

1. Mix Cajun seasoning, paprika, and cayenne pepper.
2. Coat chicken with the spice mixture and pan-sear till done.
3. Sauté spinach till wilted.

Per serving: Calories: 171kcal; Fat: 3gm; Carbs: 6gm; Protein: 30gm; Sugar: 1gm; Sodium: 200mg; Potassium: 310mg

CHAPTER 8. BEEF RECIPES

91. Beef Stir-Fry with Broccoli and Bell Peppers

Preparation time: 15 mins
Cooking time: 15 mins
Servings: 2
Ingredients:

- 8 oz. lean beef sirloin, finely cut
- 2 teacups broccoli florets
- 1 red bell pepper, sliced
- 1 green bell pepper, sliced
- 2 pieces garlic, crushed
- 1 tsp low-sodium soy sauce
- 1 tsp olive oil
- Black pepper as required

Directions:

1. Warm olive oil in your skillet in a med-high temp.
2. Include beef and garlic, cook till browned.
3. Include broccoli and bell peppers, stir-fry till tender.
4. Include soy sauce and black pepper.
5. Serve hot.

Per serving: Calories: 321kcal; Fat: 8gm; Carbs: 25gm; Protein: 32gm; Sugar: 8gm; Sodium: 150mg; Potassium: 558mg

92. Beef and Vegetable Kabobs

Preparation time: 20 mins
Cooking time: 10 mins
Servings: 2
Ingredients:

- 8 oz. lean beef tenderloin, cubed
- 1 zucchini, sliced
- 1 red onion, cut into chunks
- 1 red bell pepper, cut into chunks
- 1 yellow bell pepper, cut into chunks
- 1 tsp olive oil
- 1 tsp dried oregano
- 1 tsp dried thyme

Directions:

1. Thread beef and vegetables onto skewers.
2. Brush using olive oil then spray with herbs.
3. Grill or broil till beef is cooked to desired doneness.
4. Serve hot.

Per serving: Calories: 288kcal; Fat: 6gm; Carbs: 25gm; Protein: 32gm; Sugar: 10gm; Sodium: 10mg; Potassium: 567mg

93. Beef and Spinach Salad

Preparation time: 15 mins

Cooking time: 5 mins

Servings: 2

Ingredients:

- 8 oz. lean beef sirloin, sliced
- 4 teacups fresh spinach leaves
- 1 teacup cherry tomatoes, halved
- 1/4 red onion, finely cut
- 1/4 teacup balsamic vinaigrette dressing (low-sodium)

Directions:

1. Cook beef in your griddle in a med-high temp. till browned.
2. Inside your container, blend spinach, cherry tomatoes, and red onion.
3. Top with cooked beef.
4. Spray with balsamic vinaigrette.
5. Toss and serve.

Per serving: Calories: 308kcal; Fat: 10gm; Carbs: 14gm; Protein: 36gm; Sugar: 8gm; Sodium: 150mg; Potassium: 621mg

94. Beef and Mushroom Stuffed Bell Peppers

Preparation time: 30 mins

Cooking time: 40 mins

Servings: 2

Ingredients:

- 2 bell peppers, halved and seeds removed
- 8 oz. lean ground beef
- 1 teacup mushrooms, severed
- 1/2 teacup cubed tomatoes (no added salt)
- 1/2 teacup quinoa, cooked
- 1/2 tsp dried basil
- 1/2 tsp dried oregano

Directions:

1. Warm up oven to 375 deg.F.
2. Inside a griddle, brown beef and mushrooms.
3. Stir in tomatoes, quinoa, and herbs.
4. Stuff bell pepper halves with the beef mixture.
5. Bake for 30-40 mins 'til peppers are tender.

Per serving: Calories: 353kcal; Fat: 12gm; Carbs: 30gm; Protein: 28gm; Sugar: 6gm; Sodium: 30mg; Potassium: 621mg

95. Beef and Asparagus Stir-Fry

Preparation time: 15 mins

Cooking time: 15 mins

Servings: 2

Ingredients:

- 8 oz. lean beef tenderloin, finely cut
- 1 bunch asparagus, clipped then cut into 2-inch pieces
- 1 carrot, finely cut
- 2 pieces garlic, crushed
- 1 tsp low-sodium soy sauce

- 1 tsp olive oil
- Black pepper as required

Directions:
1. Warm olive oil in your skillet in a med-high temp.
2. Include beef and garlic, cook till browned.
3. Include asparagus and carrot, stir-fry till tender.
4. Include soy sauce and black pepper.
5. Serve hot.

Per serving: Calories: 288kcal; Fat: 8gm; Carbs: 14gm; Protein: 36gm; Sugar: 6gm; Sodium: 150mg; Potassium: 687mg

96. Beef and Bean Chili

Preparation time: 20 mins
Cooking time: 30 mins
Servings: 2
Ingredients:

- 8 oz. lean ground beef
- 1 tin (15 oz.) kidney beans, that is drained and washed (low-sodium)
- 1 tin (15 oz.) cubed tomatoes (no added salt)
- 1/2 onion, cubed
- 2 pieces garlic, crushed
- 1 tsp chili powder
- 1/2 tsp cumin
- 1/2 tsp paprika

Directions:
1. Inside a pot, brown beef with onions and garlic.
2. Include kidney beans, cubed tomatoes, and spices.
3. Simmer for 20-30 mins.
4. Serve hot.

Per serving: Calories: 351kcal; Fat: 10gm; Carbs: 38gm; Protein: 28gm; Sugar: 8gm; Sodium: 30mg; Potassium: 574mg

97. Beef and Spinach Stuffed Portobello Mushrooms

Preparation time: 20 mins
Cooking time: 20 mins
Servings: 2
Ingredients:

- 2 large portobello mushrooms, stems removed
- 8 oz. lean ground beef
- 2 teacups fresh spinach, severed
- 1/2 teacup cubed tomatoes (no added salt)
- 1/4 teacup cubed red bell pepper
- 1/4 teacup cubed onion
- 1 tsp dried basil

Directions:
1. Warm up oven to 375 deg.F.
2. Inside a griddle, brown beef with onions and red pepper.

3. Stir in spinach, cubed tomatoes, and basil.
4. Spoon beef mixture into mushroom caps.
5. Bake for 20 mins.

Per serving: Calories: 329kcal; Fat: 14gm; Carbs: 14gm; Protein: 32gm; Sugar: 6gm; Sodium: 40mg; Potassium: 415mg

98. Beef and Green Bean Stir-Fry

Preparation time: 15 mins
Cooking time: 15 mins
Servings: 2
Ingredients:

- 8 oz. lean beef tenderloin, finely cut
- 2 teacups fresh green beans, that is clipped and halved
- 1 red bell pepper, sliced
- 2 pieces garlic, crushed
- 1 tsp low-sodium soy sauce
- 1 tsp olive oil
- Black pepper as required

Directions:

1. Warm olive oil in your skillet in a med-high temp.
2. Include beef and garlic, cook till browned.
3. Include green beans and red pepper, stir-fry till soft.
4. Include soy sauce and black pepper.
5. Serve hot.

Per serving: Calories: 285kcal; Fat: 8gm; Carbs: 16gm; Protein: 36gm; Sugar: 8gm; Sodium: 150mg; Potassium: 347mg

99. Beef and Eggplant Skillet

Preparation time: 20 mins
Cooking time: 20 mins
Servings: 2
Ingredients:

- 8 oz. lean beef sirloin, finely cut
- 1 small eggplant, cubed
- 1/2 onion, cubed
- 2 pieces garlic, crushed
- 1 tsp olive oil
- 1 tsp dried rosemary
- 1/2 tsp dried thyme

Directions:

1. Warm olive oil in your skillet in a med-high temp.
2. Include beef, garlic, and onion, cook till browned.
3. Stir in eggplant and herbs.
4. Cook till eggplant is soft.
5. Serve hot.

Per serving: Calories: 308kcal; Fat: 8gm; Carbs: 22gm; Protein: 36gm; Sugar: 8gm; Sodium: 150mg; Potassium: 589mg

100. Beef and Pea Risotto

Preparation time: 20 mins

Cooking time: 30 mins

Servings: 2

Ingredients:

- 8 oz. lean beef tenderloin, cubed
- 1 teacup Arborio rice
- 1/2 teacup frozen peas
- 1/2 onion, cubed
- 2 pieces garlic, crushed
- 2 teacups low-sodium beef broth
- 1/2 teacup dry white wine
- 1 tsp olive oil

Directions:

1. Inside a griddle, brown beef with onions and garlic.
2. Stir in Arborio rice then cook for 2 mins.
3. Include white wine then cook till absorbed.
4. Gradually include beef broth, stirring constantly.
5. Include peas then cook till rice is creamy.
6. Serve hot.

Per serving: Calories: 406kcal; Fat: 6gm; Carbs: 56g; Protein: 32gm; Sugar: 4gm; Sodium: 150mg; Potassium: 557mg

101. Beef and Mushroom Lettuce Wraps

Preparation time: 20 mins

Cooking time: 15 mins

Servings: 2

Ingredients:

- 8 oz. lean ground beef
- 1 teacup mushrooms, finely severed
- 1/2 teacup cubed red bell pepper
- 1/4 teacup cubed onion
- 2 pieces garlic, crushed
- 2 tbsps low-sodium soy sauce
- 1 tsp olive oil
- Lettuce leaves for wrapping

Directions:

1. Inside a griddle, brown beef with onions, garlic, and mushrooms.
2. Include red bell pepper then cook till tender.
3. Stir in soy sauce and olive oil.
4. Serve in lettuce leaves.

Per serving: Calories: 327kcal; Fat: 16gm; Carbs: 14gm; Protein: 30gm; Sugar: 6gm; Sodium: 483mg; Potassium: 653mg

102. Beef and Cucumber Salad

Preparation time: 15 mins

Cooking time: 10 mins

Servings: 2

Ingredients:

- 8 oz. lean beef sirloin, finely cut
- 1 cucumber, finely cut
- 1/4 red onion, finely cut

- 2 tbsps rice vinegar
- 1 tsp olive oil
- 1/2 tsp dried dill

Directions:
1. Warm olive oil in your skillet in a med-high temp.
2. Include beef then cook till browned.
3. Inside your container, blend cucumber, red onion, rice vinegar, and dried dill.
4. Top with cooked beef.
5. Serve cold.

Per serving: Calories: 284kcal; Fat: 8gm; Carbs: 12gm; Protein: 36gm; Sugar: 4gm; Sodium: 153mg; Potassium: 587mg

103. Beef and Sweet Potato Hash

Preparation time: 20 mins
Cooking time: 20 mins
Servings: 2
Ingredients:

- 8 oz. lean ground beef
- 1 sweet potato, cubed
- 1/2 onion, cubed
- 2 pieces garlic, crushed
- 1 tsp olive oil
- 1/2 tsp paprika
- 1/2 tsp dried thyme

Directions:
1. Warm olive oil in your skillet in a med-high temp.
2. Include beef, garlic, and onion, cook till browned.
3. Stir in sweet potato and spices.
4. Cook till sweet potato is tender.
5. Serve hot.

Per serving: Calories: 354kcal; Fat: 14gm; Carbs: 30gm; Protein: 28gm; Sugar: 8gm; Sodium: 30mg; Potassium: 452mg

104. Beef and Tomato Quinoa Bowl

Preparation time: 20 mins
Cooking time: 15 mins
Servings: 2
Ingredients:

- 8 oz. lean beef tenderloin, finely cut
- 1 teacup cooked quinoa
- 1 teacup cherry tomatoes, halved
- 1/4 teacup cubed red onion
- 2 pieces garlic, crushed
- 1 tsp olive oil
- 1/2 tsp dried basil
- 1/2 tsp dried oregano

Directions:
1. Warm olive oil in your skillet in a med-high temp.
2. Include beef and garlic, cook till browned.

3. Inside your container, blend quinoa, cherry tomatoes, red onion, basil, and oregano.
4. Top with cooked beef.
5. Serve hot.

Per serving: Calories: 326kcal; Fat: 8gm; Carbs: 38gm; Protein: 28gm; Sugar: 6gm; Sodium: 31mg; Potassium: 570mg

105. Beef and Cauliflower Rice Bowl

Preparation time: 15 mins
Cooking time: 15 mins
Servings: 2
Ingredients:

- 8 oz. lean beef tenderloin, cubed
- 2 teacups cauliflower rice
- 1/2 teacup cubed bell peppers
- 1/4 teacup cubed red onion
- 2 pieces garlic, crushed
- 1 tsp low-sodium soy sauce
- 1 tsp olive oil
- Black pepper as required

Directions:

1. Warm olive oil in your skillet in a med-high temp.
2. Include beef, garlic, and onion, cook till browned.
3. Include cauliflower rice and bell peppers, stir-fry till tender.
4. Include soy sauce and black pepper.
5. Serve hot.

Per serving: Calories: 283kcal; Fat: 8gm; Carbs: 16gm; Protein: 36gm; Sugar: 6gm; Sodium: 150mg; Potassium: 652mg

CHAPTER 9. VEGETABLES AND GRAINS RECIPES

106. Lentil and Vegetable Soup

Preparation time: 15 mins

Cooking time: 30 mins

Servings: 2

Ingredients:

- 1/2 teacup dry green lentils
- 1 carrot, cubed
- 1 celery stalk, severed
- 1/2 onion, cubed
- 1 piece garlic, crushed
- 1 bay leaf
- 4 teacups low-sodium vegetable broth
- 1/2 teacup cubed tomatoes (canned, no added salt)

Directions:

1. Inside a pot, sauté onion and garlic till fragrant.
2. Include lentils, carrot, celery, bay leaf, and vegetable broth. Raise to a boil.
3. Decrease heat then simmer for 25 mins.
4. Include cubed tomatoes then cook for an extra 5 mins.
5. Take out bay leaf prior to serving.

Per serving: Calories: 251kcal; Fat: 1gm; Carbs: 49gm; Protein: 16gm; Sugar: 6gm; Sodium: 100mg; Potassium: 672mg

107. Quinoa-Stuffed Bell Peppers

Preparation time: 20 mins

Cooking time: 25 mins

Servings: 2

Ingredients:

- 2 bell peppers, halved and seeded
- 1/2 teacup quinoa, washed
- 1 teacup low-sodium vegetable broth
- 1 teacup cubed tomatoes (canned, no added salt)
- 1/2 teacup black beans (canned, no salt added)
- 1/2 teacup corn kernels (frozen or fresh)
- 1/2 tsp chili powder
- 1/2 tsp cumin

Directions:

1. Warm up oven to 375 deg.F.
2. Inside a pot, blend quinoa, vegetable broth, cubed tomatoes, black beans, corn, and spices.
3. Simmer for 15 mins 'til quinoa is cooked.

4. Stuff the bell peppers using the quinoa mixture.
5. Bake for 20-25 mins 'til peppers are tender.

Per serving: Calories: 356kcal; Fat: 2gm; Carbs: 71gm; Protein: 13gm; Sugar: 7gm; Sodium: 80mg; Potassium: 463mg

108. Mushroom and Spinach Risotto

Preparation time: 10 mins
Cooking time: 25 mins
Servings: 2
Ingredients:

- 1 teacup Arborio rice
- 2 teacups low-sodium vegetable broth
- 1 teacup mushrooms, sliced
- 2 teacups fresh spinach
- 1/2 onion, finely severed
- 1 piece garlic, crushed
- 1/4 teacup white wine (optional)

Directions:

1. In a pan, sauté onion and garlic till translucent.
2. Include Arborio rice then cook for 2 mins.
3. Gradually include vegetable broth, stirring constantly.
4. Include mushrooms and continue to cook till rice is creamy and mushrooms are tender.
5. Stir in fresh spinach till wilted.

Per serving: Calories: 355kcal; Fat: 1gm; Carbs: 77gm; Protein: 8gm; Sugar: 3gm; Sodium: 80mg; Potassium: 453mg

109. Roasted Veggie and Chickpea Bowl

Preparation time: 15 mins
Cooking time: 30 mins
Servings: 2
Ingredients:

- 1 teacup chickpeas (canned, no salt added), that is drained and washed
- 2 teacups mixed vegetables (e.g., bell peppers, zucchini, cherry tomatoes)
- 1 tbsp olive oil
- 1 tsp dried oregano
- 1/2 tsp paprika
- 1/2 tsp black pepper

Directions:

1. Warm up oven to 400 deg.F.
2. Toss chickpeas and mixed vegetables with olive oil and seasonings.
3. Roast in the oven for 25-30 mins, till vegetables are soft.

Per serving: Calories: 358kcal; Fat: 8gm; Carbs: 57gm; Protein: 13gm; Sugar: 9gm; Sodium: 50mg; Potassium: 643mg

110. Brown Rice and Vegetable Stir-Fry

Preparation time: 15 mins
Cooking time: 20 mins
Servings: 2
Ingredients:

- 1 teacup brown rice, cooked
- 1 teacup broccoli florets
- 1 teacup snow peas
- 1 carrot, sliced
- 1/2 red bell pepper, sliced
- 1/4 teacup low-sodium soy sauce
- 1 tbsp rice vinegar
- 1 tsp ginger, crushed
- 1 tsp garlic, crushed
- 1 tsp honey (optional)

Directions:

1. In your wok or large pan, stir-fry vegetables till tender-crisp.
2. Inside your small container, whisk collectively soy sauce, rice vinegar, ginger, garlic, and honey (if using).
3. Include cooked brown rice and sauce to the pan, tossing to blend.

Per serving: Calories: 324kcal; Fat: 2gm; Carbs: 70gm; Protein: 10gm; Sugar: 9gm; Sodium: 423mg; Potassium: 471mg

111. Spinach and Mushroom Oatmeal

Preparation time: 10 mins
Cooking time: 15 mins
Servings: 2
Ingredients:

- 1 teacup rolled oats
- 2 teacups low-sodium vegetable broth
- 2 teacups fresh spinach
- 1 teacup mushrooms, sliced
- 1/2 onion, finely severed
- 1 piece garlic, crushed
- 1/2 tsp dried thyme

Directions:

1. Inside a pot, sauté onion and garlic till translucent.
2. Include rolled oats then cook for 2 mins.
3. Gradually include vegetable broth, stirring constantly.
4. Stir in mushrooms and thyme, simmer for 10 mins.
5. Just prior to serving, stir in fresh spinach till wilted.

Per serving: Calories: 305kcal; Fat: 5gm; Carbs: 55gm; Protein: 12gm; Sugar: 3gm; Sodium: 251mg; Potassium: 453mg

112. Greek Salad

Preparation time: 10 mins

Cooking time: 0 mins

Servings: 2

Ingredients:

- 1 cucumber, cubed
- 1 tomato, cubed
- 1/4 red onion, finely cut
- 1/4 teacup Kalamata olives, that is pitted and sliced
- 2 tbsps fresh lemon juice
- 1 tbsp extra-virgin olive oil
- 1/2 tsp dried oregano

Directions:

1. Inside your container, blend cucumber, tomato, red onion, and Kalamata olives.
2. Pour with fresh lemon juice and extra-virgin olive oil.
3. Sprinkle with dried oregano then toss to blend.

Per serving: Calories: 116kcal; Fat: 7gm; Carbs: 11gm; Protein: 2gm; Sugar: 4gm; Sodium: 200mg; Potassium: 350mg

113. Cauliflower and Chickpea Curry

Preparation time: 15 mins

Cooking time: 25 mins

Servings: 2

Ingredients:

- 2 teacups cauliflower florets
- 1 teacup chickpeas (canned, no salt added), that is drained and washed
- 1/2 onion, finely severed
- 1 piece garlic, crushed
- 1 tsp ginger, crushed
- 1 tsp curry powder
- 1/2 tsp cumin
- 1/2 tsp coriander
- 1/2 teacup low-sodium vegetable broth
- 1/2 teacup canned coconut milk (light)

Directions:

1. In a pan, sauté onion, garlic, and ginger till fragrant.
2. Include cauliflower and spices, cook for 2 mins.
3. Place in vegetable broth and coconut milk, raise to a simmer.
4. Include chickpeas then simmer for an extra 15-20 mins till cauliflower is soft.

Per serving: Calories: 327kcal; Fat: 9gm; Carbs: 50gm; Protein: 10gm; Sugar: 7gm; Sodium: 180mg; Potassium: 651mg

114. Zucchini Noodles with Tomato Sauce

Preparation time: 15 mins

Cooking time: 15 mins

Servings: 2

Ingredients:

- 2 large zucchinis, spiralized into noodles
- 1 teacup cubed tomatoes (canned, no added salt)
- 1/2 onion, finely severed
- 1 piece garlic, crushed
- 1/2 tsp dried basil
- 1/2 tsp dried oregano
- 1/2 tsp red pepper flakes (optional)

Directions:

1. In a pan, sauté onion and garlic till translucent.
2. Include cubed tomatoes, basil, oregano, and red pepper flakes (if using). Simmer for 10 mins.
3. Include zucchini noodles then cook for an extra 3-5 mins till tender.

Per serving: Calories: 113kcal; Fat: 1gm; Carbs: 25gm; Protein: 4gm; Sugar: 9gm; Sodium: 60mg; Potassium: 621mg

115. Spaghetti Squash Primavera

Preparation time: 15 mins

Cooking time: 40 mins

Servings: 2

Ingredients:

- 1 small spaghetti squash
- 1 teacup cherry tomatoes, halved
- 1 teacup broccoli florets
- 1/2 red bell pepper, sliced
- 1/2 teacup sliced mushrooms
- 1/4 teacup cubed onion
- 2 pieces garlic, crushed
- 2 tbsps olive oil
- 1/2 tsp dried basil
- 1/2 tsp dried oregano
- 1/4 tsp black pepper

Directions:

1. Warm up oven to 375 deg.F.
2. Cut the spaghetti squash in ½ lengthwise, scoop out seeds, and place cut side down on your baking sheet. Roast for 30-40 mins till tender.
3. In a pan, sauté onion and garlic in olive oil till fragrant.
4. Include cherry tomatoes, broccoli, bell pepper, mushrooms, and seasonings. Cook till vegetables are tender.
5. Scrape the flesh of your spaghetti squash into strands then toss with the vegetable mixture.

Per serving: Calories: 253kcal; Fat: 10gm; Carbs: 40gm; Protein: 5gm; Sugar: 10gm; Sodium: 50mg; Potassium: 586mg

116. Cabbage and Black Bean Tacos

Preparation time: 15 mins

Cooking time: 15 mins

Servings: 2

Ingredients:

- 4 large cabbage leaves
- 1 teacup black beans (canned, no salt added), that is drained and washed
- 1/2 teacup cubed tomatoes (canned, no added salt)
- 1/2 teacup corn kernels (frozen or fresh)
- 1/2 tsp chili powder
- 1/2 tsp cumin
- 1/2 tsp paprika
- 1/4 tsp black pepper
- Salsa and avocado slices for topping (optional)

Directions:

1. In a pan, blend black beans, cubed tomatoes, corn, and spices. Cook till heated through.
2. Carefully blanch cabbage leaves in boiling water for 2 mins to soften.
3. Fill each cabbage leaf with the black bean mixture and top with salsa and avocado slices if anticipated.

Per serving: Calories: 251kcal; Fat: 2gm; Carbs: 50gm; Protein: 10gm; Sugar: 7gm; Sodium: 30mg; Potassium: 453mg

117. Sweet Potato and Chickpea Hash

Preparation time: 15 mins

Cooking time: 20 mins

Servings: 2

Ingredients:

- 1 large sweet potato, skinned and cubed
- 1 teacup chickpeas (canned, no salt added), that is drained and washed
- 1/2 red bell pepper, cubed
- 1/2 onion, cubed
- 1 piece garlic, crushed
- 1/2 tsp paprika
- 1/4 tsp cayenne pepper (as required)
- 1/4 tsp black pepper
- 1 tbsp olive oil

Directions:

1. Inside a griddle, heat olive oil and sauté onion and garlic till fragrant.
2. Include sweet potato, paprika, cayenne pepper, and black pepper. Cook till sweet potato is tender.
3. Stir in chickpeas and red bell pepper, cook for an extra 5 mins.

Per serving: Calories: 306kcal; Fat: 7gm; Carbs: 54gm; Protein: 9gm; Sugar: 10gm; Sodium: 40mg; Potassium: 672mg

118. Quinoa and Asparagus Salad

Preparation time: 15 mins

Cooking time: 15 mins

Servings: 2

Ingredients:

- 1 teacup quinoa, cooked
- 1 teacup asparagus spears, clipped and blanched
- 1/2 teacup cherry tomatoes, halved
- 1/4 teacup cubed red onion
- 2 tbsps lemon juice
- 1 tbsp olive oil
- 1/4 tsp black pepper
- Fresh basil leaves for garnish

Directions:

1. Inside your container, blend cooked quinoa, blanched asparagus, cherry tomatoes, and cubed red onion.
2. Inside your small container, whisk collectively lemon juice, olive oil, and black pepper. Pour over the quinoa mixture then toss to blend.
3. Garnish with fresh basil leaves.

Per serving: Calories: 284kcal; Fat: 8gm; Carbs: 45gm; Protein: 9gm; Sugar: 3gm; Sodium: 10mg; Potassium: 412mg

119. Stuffed Portobello Mushrooms

Preparation time: 15 mins
Cooking time: 20 mins
Servings: 2
Ingredients:

- 2 large portobello mushrooms
- 1 teacup cooked brown rice
- 1/2 teacup cubed tomatoes (canned, no added salt)
- 1/4 teacup black beans (canned, no salt added), that is drained and washed
- 1/4 teacup cubed bell pepper
- 1/4 teacup cubed onion
- 1 piece garlic, crushed
- 1/2 tsp dried oregano
- 1/4 tsp black pepper
- 2 tbsps balsamic vinegar

Directions:

1. Warm up oven to 375 deg.F.
2. Take out the stems from your portobello mushrooms and scoop out the gills.
3. Inside your container, blend cooked brown rice, cubed tomatoes, black beans, bell pepper, onion, garlic, oregano, and black pepper.
4. Stuff the mushroom caps with your rice mixture then spray with balsamic vinegar.
5. Bake for 20 mins 'til mushrooms are tender.

Per serving: Calories: 256kcal; Fat: 1gm; Carbs: 57gm; Protein: 8gm; Sugar: 9gm; Sodium: 30mg; Potassium: 661mg

120. Millet and Roasted Vegetable Salad

Preparation time: 20 mins
Cooking time: 25 mins
Servings: 2
Ingredients:

- 1 teacup millet, cooked
- 1 teacup mixed roasted vegetables (e.g., bell peppers, zucchini, eggplant)
- 1/4 teacup severed fresh parsley
- 2 tbsps lemon juice
- 1 tbsp olive oil
- 1/4 tsp black pepper
- 1/4 tsp cumin
- 1/4 tsp paprika

Directions:

1. Inside your container, blend cooked millet and mixed roasted vegetables.
2. Inside your distinct container, whisk collectively lemon juice, olive oil, black pepper, cumin, and paprika.
3. Transfer the dressing over the millet and vegetables, then toss to blend.
4. Garnish with severed fresh parsley.

Per serving: Calories: 321kcal; Fat: 7gm; Carbs: 57gm; Protein: 9gm; Sugar: 2gm; Sodium: 20mg; Potassium: 380mg

CHAPTER 10. FISH AND SHELLFISH RECIPES

121. Baked Salmon with Dill

Preparation time: 10 mins

Cooking time: 15 mins

Servings: 2

Ingredients:

- 2 salmon fillets
- 1 tbsp fresh dill, severed
- 1 lemon, juiced
- 1 tsp olive oil

Directions:

1. Warm up the oven to 400 deg.F.
2. Put salmon fillets on your baking sheet.
3. Mix dill, lemon juice, and olive oil; spray over salmon.
4. Bake for 15 mins.

Per serving: Calories: 247kcal; Fat: 12gm; Carbs: 3gm; Protein: 30gm; Sugar: 1gm; Sodium: 60mg; Potassium: 542mg

122. Poached Tilapia with Herbed Tomatoes

Preparation time: 10 mins

Cooking time: 15 mins

Servings: 2

Ingredients:

- 2 tilapia fillets
- 1 teacup cubed tomatoes
- 1/4 teacup severed fresh basil
- 1/4 teacup severed fresh parsley
- 1 garlic piece, crushed

Directions:

1. Inside a griddle, blend tomatoes, basil, parsley, and garlic.
2. Place tilapia fillets on top.
3. Simmer covered for 15 mins till fish flakes easily.

Per serving: Calories: 162kcal; Fat: 2gm; Carbs: 7gm; Protein: 30gm; Sugar: 3gm; Sodium: 50mg; Potassium: 435mg

123. Baked Herb-Crusted Snapper

Preparation time: 10 mins

Cooking time: 20 mins

Servings: 2

Ingredients:

- 2 snapper fillets
- 1/4 teacup whole wheat breadcrumbs
- 1 tsp dried thyme
- 1 tsp dried rosemary
- 1 tsp lemon zest
- 1 tsp olive oil

Directions:

1. Warm up the oven to 375 deg.F.
2. Mix breadcrumbs, thyme, rosemary, and lemon zest.

3. Coat snapper fillets with olive oil, then with breadcrumb mixture.
4. Bake for 20 mins.

Per serving: Calories: 222kcal; Fat: 5gm; Carbs: 10gm; Protein: 32gm; Sugar: 1gm; Sodium: 180mg; Potassium: 550mg

124. Grilled Swordfish with Herb Salsa

Preparation time: 10 mins

Cooking time: 10 mins

Servings: 2

Ingredients:

- 2 swordfish steaks
- 1/4 teacup severed fresh cilantro
- 1/4 teacup severed fresh mint
- 1/4 teacup severed fresh basil
- 1 lemon, juiced

Directions:

1. Warm up grill to med-high temp.
2. Grill swordfish steaks for 5 mins on all sides.
3. Mix cilantro, mint, basil, and lemon juice for the salsa.
4. Serve swordfish with herb salsa.

Per serving: Calories: 287kcal; Fat: 9gm; Carbs: 7gm; Protein: 42gm; Sugar: 2gm; Sodium: 60mg; Potassium: 548mg

125. Garlic and Herb Baked Scallops

Preparation time: 10 mins

Cooking time: 15 mins

Servings: 2

Ingredients:

- 12 large sea scallops
- 2 pieces garlic, crushed
- 1 tsp dried thyme
- 1 tsp dried rosemary
- 1 tsp olive oil

Directions:

1. Warm up the oven to 375 deg.F.
2. Inside your container, blend crushed garlic, thyme, rosemary, and olive oil.
3. Place scallops on your baking sheet, brush with the garlic herb mixture.
4. Bake for 15 mins till scallops are opaque.

Per serving: Calories: 186kcal; Fat: 3gm; Carbs: 5gm; Protein: 25gm; Sugar: 0gm; Sodium: 322mg; Potassium: 370mg

126. Shrimp and Vegetable Stir-Fry

Preparation time: 15 mins

Cooking time: 10 mins

Servings: 2

Ingredients:

- 12 big shrimp, skinned and deveined

- 2 teacups broccoli florets
- 1 bell pepper, finely cut
- 1 carrot, finely cut
- 2 pieces garlic, crushed
- 1 tbsp low-sodium soy sauce
- 1 tsp sesame oil

Directions:
1. In your wok or griddle, heat sesame oil, include garlic, and stir-fry shrimp till pink.
2. Include vegetables and stir-fry till tender-crisp.
3. Spray with soy sauce then cook for an extra min.

Per serving: Calories: 221kcal; Fat: 4gm; Carbs: 18gm; Protein: 27gm; Sugar: 5gm; Sodium: 361mg; Potassium: 670mg

127. Lemon Dill Baked Catfish

Preparation time: 10 mins
Cooking time: 20 mins
Servings: 2
Ingredients:

- 2 catfish fillets
- 1 lemon, finely cut
- 1 tbsp fresh dill, severed
- 1 tsp olive oil

Directions:
1. Warm up the oven to 375 deg.F.
2. Place catfish fillets on your baking sheet, top with lemon slices.
3. Sprinkle fresh dill then spray with olive oil.
4. Bake for 20 mins.

Per serving: Calories: 212kcal; Fat: 4gm; Carbs: 2gm; Protein: 36gm; Sugar: 0gm; Sodium: 65mg; Potassium: 581mg

128. Baked Lemon Garlic Tilapia

Preparation time: 10 mins
Cooking time: 20 mins
Servings: 2
Ingredients:

- 2 tilapia fillets
- 1 lemon, sliced
- 2 pieces garlic, crushed
- 1 tbsp olive oil
- Fresh parsley, severed
- Salt and pepper as required

Directions:
1. Warm up your oven to 375 deg.F.
2. Put tilapia fillets on your baking sheet lined using parchment paper.
3. Spray using olive oil, then spray with crushed garlic, salt, and pepper.
4. Lay lemon slices on top of the fillets.
5. Bake for 20 mins or 'til the fish flakes easily.
6. Garnish with fresh parsley prior to serving.

Per serving: Calories: 180kcal; Fat: 7gm; Carbs: 4gm; Protein: 27gm; Sugar: 2gm; Sodium: 85mg; Potassium: 435mg

129. Grilled Tuna Steak with Cucumber Salad

Preparation time: 15 mins

Cooking time: 8 mins

Servings: 2

Ingredients:

- 2 tuna steaks
- 1 cucumber, finely cut
- 1/4 teacup red onion, finely cut
- 2 tbsps fresh dill, severed
- 1 lemon, juiced
- 1 tsp olive oil

Directions:

1. Warm up grill to med-high temp.
2. Grill tuna steaks for 4 mins on all sides.
3. Inside your container, blend lemon juice, cucumber, red onion, dill, and olive oil to make your salad.
4. Serve tuna steaks with cucumber salad.

Per serving: Calories: 234kcal; Fat: 6gm; Carbs: 9gm; Protein: 34gm; Sugar: 3gm; Sodium: 80mg; Potassium: 761mg

130. Baked Garlic Butter Shrimp

Preparation time: 10 mins

Cooking time: 15 mins

Servings: 2

Ingredients:

- 12 big shrimp, skinned and deveined
- 2 pieces garlic, crushed
- 2 tbsps fresh parsley, severed
- 1 tsp olive oil

Directions:

1. Warm up the oven to 375 deg.F.
2. Inside your container, blend shrimp, crushed garlic, severed parsley, and olive oil.
3. Put shrimp on your baking sheet.
4. Bake for 15 mins 'til shrimp are pink and opaque.

Per serving: Calories: 169kcal; Fat: 4gm; Carbs: 1gm; Protein: 27gm; Sugar: 0gm; Sodium: 160mg; Potassium: 180mg

131. Sesame Crusted Salmon with Spinach

Preparation time: 10 mins

Cooking time: 15 mins

Servings: 2

Ingredients:

- 2 salmon fillets
- 2 tbsps sesame seeds
- 2 teacups fresh spinach
- 1 tsp olive oil
- 1 tsp low-sodium soy sauce

Directions:

1. Warm up the oven to 375 deg.F.
2. Coat salmon fillets with sesame seeds.
3. Bake for 15 mins 'til salmon flakes easily.
4. In a pan, sauté spinach with olive oil and soy sauce till wilted.

Per serving: Calories: 271kcal; Fat: 16gm; Carbs: 4gm; Protein: 28gm; Sugar: 0gm; Sodium: 220mg; Potassium: 693mg

132. Mediterranean Style Grilled Sardines

Preparation time: 10 mins
Cooking time: 10 mins
Servings: 2
Ingredients:

- 4 fresh sardine fillets
- 2 pieces garlic, crushed
- 1 tsp dried oregano
- 1 lemon, juiced
- 1 tsp olive oil

Directions:

1. Warm up grill to med-high temp.
2. Mix crushed garlic, dried oregano, lemon juice, and olive oil.
3. Grill sardine fillets for 5 mins on all sides, brushing with the garlic mixture.

Per serving: Calories: 185kcal; Fat: 11gm; Carbs: 2gm; Protein: 19gm; Sugar: 1gm; Sodium: 70mg; Potassium: 340mg

133. Broiled Lemon Butter Lobster Tails

Preparation time: 10 mins
Cooking time: 10 mins
Servings: 2
Ingredients:

- 2 lobster tails, split in half
- 2 tbsps lemon juice
- 2 tbsps fresh parsley, severed
- 1 tsp olive oil

Directions:

1. Warm up the broiler.
2. Mix lemon juice, severed parsley, and olive oil.
3. Brush lobster tails with the lemon mixture.
4. Broil for 5 mins, then turn then broil for an extra 5 mins.

Per serving: Calories: 141kcal; Fat: 3gm; Carbs: 1gm; Protein: 26gm; Sugar: 0gm; Sodium: 340mg; Potassium: 190mg

134. Seared Scallops with Spinach

Preparation time: 15 mins
Cooking time: 10 mins
Servings: 2

Ingredients:

- 12 scallops
- 4 teacups fresh spinach leaves
- 2 pieces garlic, crushed
- 1 tbsp olive oil
- 1 lemon, juiced
- Salt and pepper as required

Directions:

1. Warm olive oil in your skillet in a med-high temp.
2. Season scallops using salt and pepper and include them to the hot griddle.
3. Sear scallops for around 2-3 mins on all sides 'til golden brown and opaque.
4. Take out scallops from the skillet.
5. In your same skillet, include crushed garlic and sauté for around 30 secs.
6. Include fresh spinach and cook 'til wilted.
7. Spray with lemon juice.
8. Serve scallops on a bed of sautéed spinach.

Per serving: Calories: 250kcal; Fat: 9gm; Carbs: 10gm; Protein: 30gm; Sugar: 3gm; Sodium: 450mg; Potassium: 215mg

135. Baked Coconut Shrimp

Preparation time: 15 mins
Cooking time: 15 mins
Servings: 2

Ingredients:

- 12 big shrimp, skinned and deveined
- 1/2 teacup unsweetened shredded coconut
- 1/4 teacup whole wheat flour
- 1/4 teacup egg whites

Directions:

1. Warm up the oven to 375 deg.F.
2. Dredge shrimp in flour, dip in egg whites, and coat with shredded coconut.
3. Put shrimp on your baking sheet.
4. Bake for 15 mins till shrimp are golden brown.

Per serving: Calories: 198kcal; Fat: 5gm; Carbs: 18gm; Protein: 15gm; Sugar: 2gm; Sodium: 95mg; Potassium: 210mg

CHAPTER 11. SIDE RECIPES

136. Lemon Herb Quinoa

Preparation time: 10 mins

Cooking time: 15 mins

Servings: 2

Ingredients:

- 1/2 teacup quinoa
- 1 teacup low-sodium vegetable broth
- 1 lemon, zest and juice
- 1 tsp dried herbs (e.g., thyme or rosemary)

Directions:

1. Rinse quinoa under cold water.
2. Inside a saucepot, blend quinoa and vegetable broth. Raise to a boil, then decrease temp. then simmer for 15 mins.
3. Fluff quinoa using a fork and stir in lemon zest, lemon juice, and dried herbs.

Per serving: Calories: 183kcal; Fat: 1gm; Carbs: 38gm; Protein: 6gm; Sugar: 1gm; Sodium: 10mg; Potassium: 140mg

137. Garlic Roasted Brussels Sprouts

Preparation time: 10 mins

Cooking time: 20 mins

Servings: 2

Ingredients:

- 1/2 lb. Brussels sprouts, clipped and halved
- 2 pieces garlic, crushed
- 1 tbsp olive oil
- Fresh ground black pepper as required

Directions:

1. Warm up oven to 400 deg.F.
2. Toss Brussels sprouts with garlic, olive oil, and black pepper.
3. Roast for 20 mins or 'til tender, stirring halfway through.

Per serving: Calories: 95kcal; Fat: 5gm; Carbs: 10gm; Protein: 3gm; Sugar: 2gm; Sodium: 20mg; Potassium: 320mg

138. Roasted Asparagus

Preparation time: 10 mins

Cooking time: 15 mins

Servings: 2

Ingredients:

- 1/2 lb. asparagus, clipped
- 1 tbsp olive oil
- 1/2 lemon, zest and juice
- Salt substitute and pepper as required

Directions:

1. Warm up oven to 425 deg.F.

2. Toss asparagus with lemon zest, olive oil, lemon juice, salt substitute, and pepper.
3. Roast for 15 mins or till tender, shaking the pan occasionally.

Per serving: Calories: 45kcal; Fat: 3gm; Carbs: 5gm; Protein: 2gm; Sugar: 2gm; Sodium: 1mg; Potassium: 260mg

139. Brown Rice Pilaf

Preparation time: 10 mins
Cooking time: 45 mins
Servings: 2
Ingredients:

- 1/2 teacup brown rice
- 1 teacup low-sodium vegetable broth
- 1/4 teacup cubed carrots
- 1/4 teacup cubed bell pepper
- 1/4 teacup cubed zucchini
- 1/4 teacup cubed onion
- 1/2 tsp dried thyme

Directions:

1. Inside a saucepot, blend brown rice and vegetable broth. Boil, then decrease temp., cover, then simmer for 45 mins.
2. In a separate pan, sauté carrots, bell pepper, zucchini, and onion till tender. Stir in dried thyme.
3. Mix cooked vegetables with cooked brown rice.

Per serving: Calories: 181kcal; Fat: 1gm; Carbs: 40gm; Protein: 4gm; Sugar: 2gm; Sodium: 10mg; Potassium: 173mg

140. Steamed Green Beans with Almonds

Preparation time: 10 mins
Cooking time: 10 mins
Servings: 2
Ingredients:

- 1/2 lb. green beans, clipped
- 2 tbsps slivered almonds
- 1/2 lemon, zest and juice
- Salt substitute and pepper as required

Directions:

1. Steam green beans till tender, about 5-7 mins.
2. In a dry skillet, toast slivered almonds till lightly browned.
3. Toss steamed green beans with toasted almonds, lemon zest, lemon juice, salt substitute, and pepper.

Per serving: Calories: 66kcal; Fat: 3gm; Carbs: 7gm; Protein: 3gm; Sugar: 2gm; Sodium: 1mg; Potassium: 208mg

141. Stir-Fried Broccoli and Mushrooms

Preparation time: 10 mins
Cooking time: 10 mins
Servings: 2

Ingredients:

- 1/2 lb. broccoli florets
- 4 oz. mushrooms, sliced
- 2 pieces garlic, crushed
- 1 tbsp low-sodium soy sauce
- 1 tsp sesame oil

Directions:

1. Inside a griddle, heat sesame oil in a med-high temp.
2. Include crushed garlic and stir-fry for 30 secs.
3. Include broccoli florets and mushrooms, stir-fry for 5-7 mins till tender.
4. Stir in low-sodium soy sauce then cook for an extra 2 mins.

Per serving: Calories: 65kcal; Fat: 2gm; Carbs: 9gm; Protein: 4gm; Sugar: 2gm; Sodium: 130mg; Potassium: 441mg

142. Sautéed Spinach with Garlic

Preparation time: 5 mins
Cooking time: 5 mins
Servings: 2
Ingredients:

- 8 oz. fresh spinach leaves
- 2 pieces garlic, crushed
- 1 tsp olive oil
- Fresh ground black pepper as required

Directions:

1. Warm olive oil in your skillet in a med-high temp.
2. Include crushed garlic and sauté for 30 secs.
3. Include fresh spinach and sauté till wilted, about 3-5 mins.
4. Season with fresh ground black pepper.

Per serving: Calories: 44kcal; Fat: 2gm; Carbs: 4gm; Protein: 3gm; Sugar: 0gm; Sodium: 60mg; Potassium: 565mg

143. Herbed Brown Lentils

Preparation time: 10 mins
Cooking time: 30 mins
Servings: 2
Ingredients:

- 1/2 teacup brown lentils
- 1 1/2 teacups low-sodium vegetable broth
- 1/2 tsp dried thyme
- 1/2 tsp dried rosemary

Directions:

1. Rinse lentils under cold water.
2. Inside a saucepot, blend lentils, vegetable broth, dried thyme, and dried rosemary. Raise to a boil.
3. Decrease heat, cover, then simmer for 25-30 mins or till lentils are soft.

Per serving: Calories: 158kcal; Fat: 0gm; Carbs: 27gm; Protein: 9gm; Sugar: 1gm; Sodium: 5mg; Potassium: 464mg

144. Grilled Eggplant

Preparation time: 10 mins

Cooking time: 10 mins

Servings: 2

Ingredients:

- 1 medium eggplant, sliced into rounds
- 1 tbsp olive oil
- 1/2 tsp dried basil
- 1/2 tsp dried oregano

Directions:

1. Warm up grill to med-high temp.
2. Brush eggplant slices using olive oil then spray with dried basil and dried oregano.
3. Grill for 4-5 mins on all sides till tender and grill marks appear.

Per serving: Calories: 84kcal; Fat: 4gm; Carbs: 11gm; Protein: 1gm; Sugar: 4gm; Sodium: 0mg; Potassium: 343mg

145. Sautéed Snow Peas with Lemon

Preparation time: 10 mins

Cooking time: 5 mins

Servings: 2

Ingredients:

- 8 oz. snow peas, clipped
- 1 lemon, zest and juice
- 1 tsp olive oil
- Salt substitute and pepper as required

Directions:

1. Warm olive oil in your skillet in a med-high temp.
2. Include snow peas and sauté for 3-5 mins till tender-crisp.
3. Stir in lemon zest, lemon juice, salt substitute, and pepper.

Per serving: Calories: 45kcal; Fat: 1gm; Carbs: 7gm; Protein: 2gm; Sugar: 2gm; Sodium: 0mg; Potassium: 140mg

146. Roasted Red Pepper Hummus

Preparation time: 10 mins

Cooking time: 0 mins

Servings: 2

Ingredients:

- 1 tin (15 oz.) chickpeas, that is drained and washed
- 1/2 teacup roasted red peppers, drained
- 1 piece garlic
- 2 tbsps tahini
- Juice of 1 lemon
- 1/2 tsp ground cumin

Directions:

1. Inside your blending container, blend chickpeas, roasted red peppers,

garlic, tahini, lemon juice, and ground cumin.

2. Blend 'til smooth, scraping down the sides as needed.

Per serving: Calories: 151kcal; Fat: 7gm; Carbs: 18gm; Protein: 6gm; Sugar: 3gm; Sodium: 190mg; Potassium: 225mg

147. Cauliflower "Mashed Potatoes"

Preparation time: 10 mins
Cooking time: 20 mins
Servings: 2
Ingredients:

- 1/2 head cauliflower, cut into florets
- 2 pieces garlic, crushed
- 1/4 teacup low-sodium vegetable broth
- Fresh chives, severed for garnish

Directions:

1. Steam cauliflower florets till very tender, about 10-15 mins.
2. In your blender or your food processor, blend steamed cauliflower, crushed garlic, and vegetable broth. Blend till smooth.
3. Garnish with fresh chives.

Per serving: Calories: 56kcal; Fat: 0gm; Carbs: 10gm; Protein: 3gm; Sugar: 3gm; Sodium: 30mg; Potassium: 460mg

148. Sautéed Swiss Chard

Preparation time: 10 mins
Cooking time: 10 mins
Servings: 2
Ingredients:

- 8 oz. Swiss chard, severed
- 2 pieces garlic, crushed
- 1 tsp olive oil
- 1/2 tsp red pepper flakes (optional)
- Salt substitute and pepper as required

Directions:

1. Warm olive oil in your griddle in a med-high temp.
2. Place crushed garlic and red pepper flakes (if using) then sauté for 30 secs.
3. Include severed Swiss chard and sauté for 5-7 mins till wilted.
4. Season with salt substitute and pepper.

Per serving: Calories: 31kcal; Fat: 1gm; Carbs: 5gm; Protein: 2gm; Sugar: 1gm; Sodium: 120mg; Potassium: 292mg

149. Roasted Cauliflower with Turmeric

Preparation time: 10 mins
Cooking time: 25 mins
Servings: 2
Ingredients:

- 1/2 head cauliflower, cut into florets

- 1 tbsp olive oil
- 1/2 tsp turmeric
- 1/2 tsp paprika
- 1/2 tsp cumin

Directions:

1. Warm up oven to 425 deg.F.
2. Toss cauliflower florets with olive oil, turmeric, paprika, and cumin.
3. Disperse on your baking sheet in a single layer then roast for 25 mins or till soft and golden.

Per serving: Calories: 73kcal; Fat: 3gm; Carbs: 10gm; Protein: 3gm; Sugar: 3gm; Sodium: 30mg; Potassium: 481mg

150. Avocado and Tomato Salad

Preparation time: 10 mins
Cooking time: 0 mins
Servings: 2
Ingredients:

- 1 avocado, cubed
- 1 tomato, cubed
- 1/4 red onion, finely cut
- 2 tbsps fresh cilantro, severed
- Juice of 1 lime
- Salt substitute and pepper as required

Directions:

1. Inside your container, blend cubed avocado, cubed tomato, finely cut red onion, and fresh cilantro.
2. Spray with lime juice then season with salt substitute and pepper.

Per serving: Calories: 167kcal; Fat: 13gm; Carbs: 12gm; Protein: 2gm; Sugar: 2gm; Sodium: 0mg; Potassium: 583mg

CHAPTER 12. SOUPS RECIPES

151. Vegetable Quinoa Soup

Preparation time: 15 mins

Cooking time: 30 mins

Servings: 2

Ingredients:

- 1/2 teacup quinoa
- 2 teacups low-sodium vegetable broth
- 1 teacup cubed carrots
- 1 teacup cubed zucchini
- 1 teacup cubed tomatoes
- 1/2 teacup cubed bell peppers
- 1/2 tsp black pepper
- 1 tsp dried thyme

Directions:

1. Rinse quinoa thoroughly.
2. Inside a pot, blend quinoa, vegetable broth, and vegetables.
3. Simmer for 25-30 mins 'til vegetables are tender.
4. Season with black pepper and thyme.

Per serving: Calories: 305kcal; Fat: 2gm; Carbs: 63gm; Protein: 9gm; Sugar: 6gm; Sodium: 150mg; Potassium: 726mg

152. Chickpea and Vegetable Soup

Preparation time: 15 mins

Cooking time: 25 mins

Servings: 2

Ingredients:

- 1 tin (15 oz.) low-sodium chickpeas, drained
- 2 teacups low-sodium vegetable broth
- 1 teacup cubed sweet potatoes
- 1 teacup cubed celery
- 1 teacup cubed bell peppers
- 1/2 tsp cayenne pepper
- 1/2 tsp turmeric

Directions:

1. Inside a pot, blend chickpeas, vegetable broth, sweet potatoes, celery, and bell peppers.
2. Simmer for 20 mins.
3. Season with cayenne pepper and turmeric.

Per serving: Calories: 324kcal; Fat: 2gm; Carbs: 63gm; Protein: 14gm; Sugar: 10gm; Sodium: 180mg; Potassium: 675mg

153. Broccoli and White Bean Soup

Preparation time: 10 mins

Cooking time: 25 mins

Servings: 2

Ingredients:

- 2 teacups low-sodium vegetable broth
- 1 teacup severed broccoli

- 1 teacup canned white beans, drained
- 1/2 teacup cubed onions
- 1/2 teacup cubed celery
- 1/2 tsp garlic powder
- 1/2 tsp dried thyme

Directions:
1. Inside a pot, blend vegetable broth, broccoli, white beans, onions, and celery.
2. Simmer for 20 mins.
3. Season with garlic powder and thyme.

Per serving: Calories: 227kcal; Fat: 1gm; Carbs: 43gm; Protein: 13gm; Sugar: 5gm; Sodium: 220mg; Potassium: 546mg

154. Spinach and Mushroom Soup

Preparation time: 10 mins
Cooking time: 25 mins
Servings: 2
Ingredients:
- 2 teacups low-sodium vegetable broth
- 2 teacups fresh spinach
- 1 teacup sliced mushrooms
- 1/2 teacup cubed onions
- 1/2 tsp black pepper
- 1/2 tsp dried thyme

Directions:
1. Inside a pot, blend vegetable broth, spinach, mushrooms, and onions.
2. Simmer for 20 mins.
3. Season with black pepper and thyme.

Per serving: Calories: 88kcal; Fat: 1gm; Carbs: 17gm; Protein: 5gm; Sugar: 3gm; Sodium: 251mg; Potassium: 682mg

155. Asparagus and Lemon Soup

Preparation time: 10 mins
Cooking time: 20 mins
Servings: 2
Ingredients:
- 2 teacups low-sodium vegetable broth
- 1 teacup severed asparagus
- 1/2 teacup cubed onions
- 1/2 teacup severed leeks
- Zest and juice of 1 lemon
- 1/2 tsp black pepper

Directions:
1. Inside a pot, blend vegetable broth, asparagus, onions, and leeks.
2. Simmer for 15 mins.
3. Stir in lemon zest, lemon juice, and black pepper.

Per serving: Calories: 96kcal; Fat: 0gm; Carbs: 22gm; Protein: 3gm; Sugar: 7gm; Sodium: 183mg; Potassium: 591mg

156. Sweet Potato and Black Bean Soup

Preparation time: 15 mins
Cooking time: 30 mins

Servings: 2

Ingredients:

- 2 teacups low-sodium vegetable broth
- 1 teacup cubed sweet potatoes
- 1 teacup canned black beans, drained
- 1/2 teacup cubed onions
- 1/2 teacup cubed red bell peppers
- 1/2 tsp chili powder
- 1/2 tsp cumin

Directions:

1. Inside a pot, blend vegetable broth, sweet potatoes, black beans, onions, and red bell peppers.
2. Simmer for 25 mins.
3. Season with chili powder and cumin.

Per serving: Calories: 271kcal; Fat: 1gm; Carbs: 54gm; Protein: 11gm; Sugar: 6gm; Sodium: 240mg; Potassium: 460mg

157. Cauliflower and Turmeric Soup

Preparation time: 10 mins

Cooking time: 25 mins

Servings: 2

Ingredients:

- 2 teacups low-sodium vegetable broth
- 1 teacup severed cauliflower
- 1/2 teacup cubed onions
- 1/2 teacup cubed celery
- 1/2 tsp turmeric
- 1/2 tsp black pepper

Directions:

1. Inside a pot, blend vegetable broth, cauliflower, onions, and celery.
2. Simmer for 20 mins.
3. Season with turmeric and black pepper.

Per serving: Calories: 98kcal; Fat: 0gm; Carbs: 20gm; Protein: 3gm; Sugar: 5gm; Sodium: 210mg; Potassium: 552mg

158. Green Pea and Mint Soup

Preparation time: 10 mins

Cooking time: 25 mins

Servings: 2

Ingredients:

- 2 teacups low-sodium vegetable broth
- 1 teacup green peas (fresh or frozen)
- 1/2 teacup cubed onions
- 1/2 teacup severed fresh mint leaves
- 1/2 tsp black pepper
- 1/2 tsp garlic powder

Directions:

1. Inside a pot, blend vegetable broth, green peas, onions, and mint leaves.
2. Simmer for 20 mins.
3. Season with black pepper and garlic powder.

Per serving: Calories: 116kcal; Fat: 0gm; Carbs: 23gm; Protein: 4gm; Sugar: 7gm; Sodium: 230mg; Potassium: 453mg

159. Spinach and Red Lentil Soup

Preparation time: 15 mins

Cooking time: 30 mins

Servings: 2

Ingredients:

- 2 teacups low-sodium vegetable broth
- 1 teacup red lentils
- 2 teacups fresh spinach
- 1/2 teacup cubed onions
- 1/2 tsp cumin
- 1/2 tsp paprika

Directions:

1. Inside a pot, blend vegetable broth, red lentils, onions, and spices.
2. Simmer for 25 mins.
3. Stir in fresh spinach then cook till wilted.

Per serving: Calories: 325kcal; Fat: 1gm; Carbs: 59g; Protein: 20gm; Sugar: 4gm; Sodium: 180mg; Potassium: 643mg

160. Zucchini and Basil Soup

Preparation time: 10 mins

Cooking time: 25 mins

Servings: 2

Ingredients:

- 2 teacups low-sodium vegetable broth
- 1 teacup cubed zucchini
- 1/2 teacup cubed onions
- 1/2 teacup severed fresh basil leaves
- 1/2 tsp black pepper
- 1/2 tsp dried thyme

Directions:

1. Inside a pot, blend vegetable broth, zucchini, onions, and basil.
2. Simmer for 20 mins.
3. Season with black pepper and dried thyme.

Per serving: Calories: 85kcal; Fat: 0gm; Carbs: 17gm; Protein: 3gm; Sugar: 5gm; Sodium: 230mg; Potassium: 522mg

161. Carrot and Ginger Soup

Preparation time: 15 mins

Cooking time: 25 mins

Servings: 2

Ingredients:

- 2 teacups low-sodium vegetable broth
- 1 teacup cubed carrots
- 1/2 teacup cubed onions
- 1/2 tsp ginger powder
- 1/2 tsp black pepper

Directions:

1. Inside a pot, blend vegetable broth, carrots, onions, ginger powder, and black pepper.
2. Simmer for 20 mins.

Per serving: Calories: 81kcal; Fat: 0gm; Carbs: 20gm; Protein: 2gm; Sugar: 8gm; Sodium: 240mg; Potassium: 631mg

162. Spicy Bell Pepper Soup

Preparation time: 15 mins

Cooking time: 30 mins

Servings: 2

Ingredients:

- 2 teacups low-sodium vegetable broth
- 1 teacup cubed red bell peppers
- 1 teacup cubed green bell peppers
- 1/2 teacup cubed onions
- 1/2 tsp chili powder
- 1/2 tsp cayenne pepper

Directions:

1. Inside a pot, blend vegetable broth, red bell peppers, green bell peppers, onions, and spices.
2. Simmer for 25 mins.

Per serving: Calories: 74kcal; Fat: 0gm; Carbs: 17gm; Protein: 2gm; Sugar: 6gm; Sodium: 180mg; Potassium: 481mg

163. Eggplant and Tomato Soup

Preparation time: 15 mins

Cooking time: 35 mins

Servings: 2

Ingredients:

- 2 teacups low-sodium vegetable broth
- 1 teacup cubed eggplant
- 1 teacup cubed tomatoes
- 1/2 teacup cubed onions
- 1/2 tsp black pepper
- 1/2 tsp dried oregano

Directions:

1. Inside a pot, blend vegetable broth, eggplant, tomatoes, onions, and spices.
2. Simmer for 30 mins.

Per serving: Calories: 96kcal; Fat: 0gm; Carbs: 21gm; Protein: 2gm; Sugar: 9gm; Sodium: 230mg; Potassium: 688mg

164. Artichoke and Spinach Soup

Preparation time: 10 mins

Cooking time: 20 mins

Servings: 2

Ingredients:

- 2 teacups low-sodium vegetable broth
- 1 teacup canned artichoke hearts, that is drained and severed
- 2 teacups fresh spinach
- 1/2 teacup cubed onions
- 1/2 tsp black pepper
- 1/2 tsp garlic powder

Directions:

1. Inside a pot, blend vegetable broth, artichoke hearts, onions, and spices.
2. Simmer for 15 mins.
3. Stir in fresh spinach then cook till wilted.

Per serving: Calories: 72kcal; Fat: 1gm; Carbs: 16gm; Protein: 3gm; Sugar: 3gm; Sodium: 200mg; Potassium: 591mg

165. Green Bean and Almond Soup

Preparation time: 15 mins
Cooking time: 30 mins
Servings: 2
Ingredients:

- 2 teacups low-sodium vegetable broth
- 1 teacup fresh green beans, that is clipped and severed
- 1/4 teacup sliced almonds
- 1/2 teacup cubed onions
- 1/2 tsp black pepper
- 1/2 tsp thyme

Directions:

1. Inside a pot, blend vegetable broth, green beans, almonds, onions, and spices.
2. Simmer for 25 mins.

Per serving: Calories: 144kcal; Fat: 5gm; Carbs: 18gm; Protein: 6gm; Sugar: 4gm; Sodium: 225mg; Potassium: 531mg

CHAPTER 13. DESSERTS RECIPES

166. Baked Apples with Cinnamon

Preparation time: 15 mins
Cooking time: 30 mins
Servings: 2
Ingredients:

- 2 apples (any variety)
- 1 tsp ground cinnamon
- 1/4 teacup severed nuts (almonds or walnuts)

Directions:

1. Warm up the oven to 350 deg.F.
2. Core the apples and place them in a baking dish.
3. Sprinkle cinnamon and severed nuts over the apples.
4. Bake for 30 mins or 'til apples are tender.

Per serving: Calories: 154kcal; Fat: 7gm; Carbs: 21gm; Protein: 2gm; Sugar: 15gm; Sodium: 0mg; Potassium: 183mg

167. Pineapple and Banana Sorbet

Preparation time: 5 mins
Cooking time: 0 mins
Servings: 2
Ingredients:

- 1 teacup frozen pineapple chunks
- 1 ripe banana
- 1/4 teacup coconut milk (unsweetened)

Directions:

1. Place frozen pineapple, banana, and coconut milk inside a mixer.
2. Blend till smooth.
3. Serve instantly as a sorbet.

Per serving: Calories: 123kcal; Fat: 3gm; Carbs: 26gm; Protein: 1gm; Sugar: 14gm; Sodium: 0mg; Potassium: 251mg

168. Chocolate Avocado Mousse

Preparation time: 10 mins
Cooking time: 0 mins
Servings: 2
Ingredients:

- 1 ripe avocado
- 2 tbsps unsweetened cocoa powder
- 2 tbsps honey or maple syrup (optional)

Directions:

1. Scoop the flesh of your avocado into a blender.
2. Include cocoa powder and sweetener (if anticipated).
3. Blend till creamy and smooth.

4. Chill in the refrigerator prior to serving.

Per serving: Calories: 187kcal; Fat: 13gm; Carbs: 18gm; Protein: 3gm; Sugar: 9gm; Sodium: 0mg; Potassium: 483mg

169. Cinnamon Baked Pears

Preparation time: 10 mins
Cooking time: 30 mins
Servings: 2
Ingredients:

- 2 ripe pears
- 1/2 tsp ground cinnamon
- 1/4 teacup severed pecans

Directions:

1. Warm up the oven to 375 deg.F.
2. Slice pears in half and remove the core.
3. Sprinkle with cinnamon and severed pecans.
4. Bake for 30 mins till tender.

Per serving: Calories: 164kcal; Fat: 8gm; Carbs: 24gm; Protein: 2gm; Sugar: 14gm; Sodium: 0mg; Potassium: 212mg

170. Mango and Raspberry Frozen Yogurt

Preparation time: 10 mins
Cooking time: 0 mins
Servings: 2
Ingredients:

- 1 teacup frozen mango chunks
- 1/2 teacup fresh raspberries
- 1 teacup Greek yogurt (low-fat)

Directions:

1. Inside a mixer, blend frozen mango, raspberries, and Greek yogurt.
2. Blend till smooth.
3. Freeze for a firmer texture or serve instantly.

Per serving: Calories: 166kcal; Fat: 2gm; Carbs: 26gm; Protein: 11gm; Sugar: 19gm; Sodium: 30mg; Potassium: 308mg

171. Fruit Salad with Honey-Lime Drizzle

Preparation time: 10 mins
Cooking time: 0 mins
Servings: 2
Ingredients:

- 1 teacup cubed pineapple
- 1 teacup cubed cantaloupe
- 1 teacup cubed kiwi
- 1 tbsp honey
- 1 tbsp lime juice

Directions:

1. Inside your container, blend pineapple, cantaloupe, and kiwi.
2. Spray with honey and lime juice, then toss to coat.

Per serving: Calories: 126kcal; Fat: 0gm; Carbs: 30gm; Protein: 2gm; Sugar: 22gm; Sodium: 20mg; Potassium: 446mg

172. Peach and Blueberry Crisp

Preparation time: 10 mins
Cooking time: 25 mins
Servings: 2
Ingredients:

- 2 ripe peaches, sliced
- 1/2 teacup blueberries
- 1/4 teacup rolled oats
- 1/4 teacup almond flour
- 1 tbsp honey

Directions:

1. Warm up the oven to 375 deg.F.
2. Inside your container, blend peaches and blueberries.
3. In an extra bowl, mix oats, almond flour, and honey to create the topping.
4. Place fruit mixture in a baking dish then spray topping over it.
5. Bake for 25 mins 'til topping is crisp and golden.

Per serving: Calories: 206kcal; Fat: 5gm; Carbs: 38gm; Protein: 4gm; Sugar: 20gm; Sodium: 0mg; Potassium: 330mg

173. Apricot and Almond Rice Pudding

Preparation time: 10 mins
Cooking time: 25 mins
Servings: 2
Ingredients:

- 1/2 teacup arborio rice
- 2 teacups unsweetened almond milk
- 1/4 teacup dried apricots, severed
- 1/4 teacup sliced almonds
- 1/2 tsp vanilla extract

Directions:

1. Inside a saucepot, blend rice and almond milk.
2. Raise to a boil, then decrease temp. then simmer for 20-25 mins, mixing irregularly 'til rice is tender.
3. Stir in dried apricots, sliced almonds, and vanilla extract.
4. Let it cool prior to serving.

Per serving: Calories: 251kcal; Fat: 7gm; Carbs: 44gm; Protein: 4gm; Sugar: 10gm; Sodium: 180mg; Potassium: 270mg

174. Coconut and Mango Chia Popsicles

Preparation time: 10 mins (plus freezing time)
Cooking time: 0 mins
Servings: 2

Ingredients:

- 1 teacup coconut milk (unsweetened)
- 1 ripe mango, skinned and cubed
- 2 tbsps chia seeds
- 1 tbsp honey (optional)

Directions:

1. Inside a mixer, blend coconut milk, cubed mango, chia seeds, and honey (if anticipated).
2. Blend till smooth.
3. Pour into popsicle molds then freeze till solid.

Per serving: Calories: 223kcal; Fat: 16gm; Carbs: 19gm; Protein: 3gm; Sugar: 13gm; Sodium: 20mg; Potassium: 280mg

175. Baked Banana with Cinnamon and Walnuts

Preparation time: 5 mins
Cooking time: 15 mins
Servings: 2
Ingredients:

- 2 ripe bananas
- 1/2 tsp ground cinnamon
- 2 tbsps severed walnuts

Directions:

1. Warm up the oven to 350 deg.F.
2. Slice bananas in half lengthwise.
3. Sprinkle with cinnamon and severed walnuts.
4. Bake for 15 mins 'til bananas are soft and toppings are golden.

Per serving: Calories: 182kcal; Fat: 7gm; Carbs: 31gm; Protein: 2gm; Sugar: 16gm; Sodium: 0mg; Potassium: 448mg

176. Frozen Yogurt Bark

Preparation time: 10 mins
Cooking time: 0 mins
Servings: 2
Ingredients:

- 1 teacup low-fat Greek yogurt
- 1/2 tsp vanilla extract
- 2 tbsps fresh berries
- 1 tbsp severed nuts (e.g., almonds or walnuts)

Directions:

1. Mix yogurt and vanilla extract.
2. Disperse yogurt mixture on a baking sheet covered with parchment paper.
3. Sprinkle fresh berries and severed nuts on top.
4. Freeze for 2 hrs, then break into pieces.

Per serving: Calories: 120; Fat: 3gm; Carbs: 14gm; Protein: 9gm; Sugar: 12gm; Sodium: 55mg; Potassium: 251mg

177. Minty Watermelon Slush

Preparation time: 5 mins
Cooking time: 0 mins

Servings: 2

Ingredients:

- 2 teacups cubed watermelon
- 1/4 teacup fresh mint leaves
- 1/2 teacup ice cubes

Directions:

1. Inside a mixer, blend watermelon, mint leaves, and ice cubes.
2. Blend till slushy.

Per serving: Calories: 58kcal; Fat: 0gm; Carbs: 13gm; Protein: 1gm; Sugar: 10gm; Sodium: 0mg; Potassium: 220mg

178. Pomegranate and Kiwi Fruit Salad

Preparation time: 10 mins

Cooking time: 0 mins

Servings: 2

Ingredients:

- 1 teacup pomegranate seeds
- 2 kiwis, skinned and sliced
- 1/2 tsp lime juice

Directions:

1. Inside your container, blend pomegranate seeds and sliced kiwi.
2. Spray with lime juice prior to serving.

Per serving: Calories: 105kcal; Fat: 1gm; Carbs: 26gm; Protein: 2gm; Sugar: 17gm; Sodium: 5mg; Potassium: 381mg

179. Cranberry and Walnut Quinoa

Preparation time: 15 mins

Cooking time: 15 mins

Servings: 2

Ingredients:

- 1/2 teacup quinoa
- 1 teacup water
- 1/4 teacup dried cranberries
- 2 tbsps severed walnuts
- 1/2 tsp ground cinnamon

Directions:

1. Rinse quinoa thoroughly under cold water.
2. In your saucepan, blend quinoa and water, and raise to a boil.
3. Decrease heat, cover, then simmer for 15 mins.
4. Stir in dried cranberries, severed walnuts, and ground cinnamon.

Per serving: Calories: 231kcal; Fat: 8gm; Carbs: 36gm; Protein: 6gm; Sugar: 9gm; Sodium: 10mg; Potassium: 260mg

180. Peach and Raspberry Smoothie

Preparation time: 5 mins

Cooking time: 0 mins

Servings: 2

Ingredients:

- 1 teacup frozen peaches
- 1/2 teacup fresh raspberries
- 1 teacup unsweetened almond milk

Directions:

1. Inside a mixer, blend frozen peaches, fresh raspberries, and almond milk.
2. Blend till smooth.
3. Serve instantly as a refreshing smoothie.

Per serving: Calories: 83kcal; Fat: 2gm; Carbs: 15gm; Protein: 1gm; Sugar: 9gm; Sodium: 120mg; Potassium: 240mg

CHAPTER 14. BONUS #1 TASTY AND QUICK INSTANT POT RECIPES FOR DELICIOUS LUNCHES AND DINNERS

181. Instant Pot Quinoa and Black Bean Bowl

Preparation time: 10 mins

Cooking time: 1 min

Servings: 2

Ingredients:

- 1 teacup quinoa, washed
- 1 tin (15 oz.) black beans, that is drained and washed
- 1 teacup low-sodium vegetable broth
- 1 tsp chili powder
- 1 tsp cumin

Directions:

1. Blend quinoa, black beans, vegetable broth, and spices in the Instant Pot.
2. Pressure cook for 1 min.
3. Serve with your favorite veggies.

Per serving: Calories: 355kcal; Fat: 3gm; Carbs: 65g; Protein: 14gm; Sugar: 2gm; Sodium: 150mg; Potassium: 486mg

182. Instant Pot Chickpea Curry

Preparation time: 15 mins

Cooking time: 10 mins

Servings: 2

Ingredients:

- 1 tin (15 oz.) chickpeas, that is drained and washed
- 1 onion, severed
- 2 pieces garlic, crushed
- 1 tsp curry powder
- 1 tsp turmeric
- 1 tsp cayenne pepper (as required)
- 1 tin (14 oz.) cubed tomatoes
- 1 teacup low-sodium vegetable broth

Directions:

1. Sauté onion and garlic in the Instant Pot.
2. Include spices, chickpeas, cubed tomatoes, and vegetable broth.
3. Pressure cook for 5 mins.
4. Serve with brown rice.

Per serving: Calories: 283kcal; Fat: 2gm; Carbs: 52gm; Protein: 13gm; Sugar: 11gm; Sodium: 305mg; Potassium: 631mg

183. Instant Pot Minestrone Soup

Preparation time: 15 mins

Cooking time: 15 mins

Servings: 2

Ingredients:

- 1/2 teacup whole wheat pasta, uncooked

- 1 carrot, cubed
- 1 celery stalk, cubed
- 1 onion, severed
- 2 pieces garlic, crushed
- 1 tin (14 oz.) cubed tomatoes
- 1 tin (15 oz.) kidney beans, that is drained and washed
- 4 teacups low-sodium vegetable broth
- 1 tsp Italian seasoning

Directions:
1. Sauté onion, garlic, carrot, and celery in the Instant Pot.
2. Include pasta, cubed tomatoes, kidney beans, vegetable broth, and Italian seasoning.
3. Pressure cook for 5 mins.
4. Serve hot.

Per serving: Calories: 301kcal; Fat: 2gm; Carbs: 63gm; Protein: 11gm; Sugar: 8gm; Sodium: 251mg; Potassium: 568mg

184. Instant Pot Red Lentil Curry

Preparation time: 15 mins
Cooking time: 10 mins
Servings: 2
Ingredients:
- 1 teacup red lentils, washed
- 1 onion, severed
- 2 pieces garlic, crushed
- 1 tsp curry powder
- 1 tsp turmeric
- 1 tin (14 oz.) cubed tomatoes
- 1 tin (14 oz.) light coconut milk
- 2 teacups low-sodium vegetable broth

Directions:
1. Sauté onion and garlic in the Instant Pot.
2. Include lentils, spices, cubed tomatoes, coconut milk, and vegetable broth.
3. Pressure cook for 5 mins.
4. Serve with brown rice.

Per serving: Calories: 381kcal; Fat: 6gm; Carbs: 61gm; Protein: 18gm; Sugar: 6gm; Sodium: 350mg; Potassium: 654mg

185. Instant Pot Black-Eyed Pea Stew

Preparation time: 15 mins
Cooking time: 10 mins
Servings: 2
Ingredients:
- 1 teacup black-eyed peas, soaked overnight
- 1 onion, severed
- 2 pieces garlic, crushed
- 1 bell pepper, cubed
- 1 tin (14 oz.) cubed tomatoes
- 1 tsp cumin
- 1 tsp paprika
- 4 teacups low-sodium vegetable broth

Directions:

1. Sauté onion, garlic, and bell pepper in the Instant Pot.
2. Include black-eyed peas, spices, cubed tomatoes, and vegetable broth.
3. Pressure cook for 8 mins.
4. Serve hot.

Per serving: Calories: 298kcal; Fat: 1gm; Carbs: 58gm; Protein: 15gm; Sugar: 10gm; Sodium: 205mg; Potassium: 671mg

186. Instant Pot Moroccan Chickpea Stew

Preparation time: 15 mins

Cooking time: 10 mins

Servings: 2

Ingredients:

- 1 tin (15 oz.) chickpeas, that is drained and washed
- 1 onion, severed
- 2 pieces garlic, crushed
- 1 carrot, cubed
- 1 bell pepper, cubed
- 1 tsp cumin
- 1 tsp paprika
- 1 tsp cinnamon
- 4 teacups low-sodium vegetable broth

Directions:

1. Sauté onion and garlic in the Instant Pot.
2. Include chickpeas, carrot, bell pepper, spices, and vegetable broth.
3. Pressure cook for 5 mins.
4. Serve with couscous.

Per serving: Calories: 289kcal; Fat: 2gm; Carbs: 56gm; Protein: 14gm; Sugar: 14gm; Sodium: 258mg; Potassium: 651mg

187. Instant Pot Brown Rice and Bean Bowl

Preparation time: 10 mins

Cooking time: 15 mins

Servings: 2

Ingredients:

- 1 teacup brown rice, washed
- 1 tin (15 oz.) black beans, that is drained and washed
- 1 teacup cubed tomatoes
- 1 tsp chili powder
- 1 tsp cumin
- 2 teacups low-sodium vegetable broth

Directions:

1. Blend brown rice, black beans, cubed tomatoes, spices, and vegetable broth in the Instant Pot.
2. Pressure cook for 10 mins.
3. Serve with salsa and avocado.

Per serving: Calories: 358kcal; Fat: 2gm; Carbs: 70gm; Protein: 14gm; Sugar: 2gm; Sodium: 150mg; Potassium: 563mg

188. Instant Pot Spinach and Lentil Curry

Preparation time: 15 mins
Cooking time: 10 mins
Servings: 2
Ingredients:

- 1 teacup green or brown lentils, washed
- 2 teacups fresh spinach
- 1 onion, severed
- 2 pieces garlic, crushed
- 1 tsp curry powder
- 1 tsp turmeric
- 1 tin (14 oz.) cubed tomatoes
- 2 teacups low-sodium vegetable broth

Directions:

1. Sauté onion and garlic in the Instant Pot.
2. Include lentils, spices, cubed tomatoes, and vegetable broth.
3. Pressure cook for 5 mins.
4. Stir in fresh spinach prior to serving.

Per serving: Calories: 324kcal; Fat: 1gm; Carbs: 60g; Protein: 20gm; Sugar: 6gm; Sodium: 300mg; Potassium: 751mg

189. Instant Pot Vegetable and Chickpea Curry

Preparation time: 15 mins
Cooking time: 10 mins
Servings: 2
Ingredients:

- 1 tin (15 oz.) chickpeas, that is drained and washed
- 2 teacups mixed vegetables (e.g., cauliflower, peas, carrots)
- 1 onion, severed
- 2 pieces garlic, crushed
- 1 tsp curry powder
- 1 tsp turmeric
- 1 tin (14 oz.) cubed tomatoes
- 2 teacups low-sodium vegetable broth

Directions:

1. Sauté onion and garlic in the Instant Pot.
2. Include chickpeas, mixed vegetables, spices, cubed tomatoes, and vegetable broth.
3. Pressure cook for 5 mins.
4. Serve with brown rice.

Per serving: Calories: 314kcal; Fat: 3gm; Carbs: 58gm; Protein: 14gm; Sugar: 13gm; Sodium: 320mg; Potassium: 651mg

190. Instant Pot Black Bean and Corn Soup

Preparation time: 15 mins
Cooking time: 15 mins
Servings: 2

Ingredients:

- 1 tin (15 oz.) black beans, that is drained and washed
- 1 teacup frozen corn
- 1 onion, severed
- 2 pieces garlic, crushed
- 1 tsp cumin
- 1 tsp chili powder
- 4 teacups low-sodium vegetable broth

Directions:

1. Sauté onion and garlic in the Instant Pot.
2. Include black beans, corn, spices, and vegetable broth.
3. Pressure cook for 10 mins.
4. Serve hot.

Per serving: Calories: 283kcal; Fat: 2gm; Carbs: 54gm; Protein: 14gm; Sugar: 3gm; Sodium: 250mg; Potassium: 656mg

191. Instant Pot Tomato and Lentil Soup

Preparation time: 10 mins

Cooking time: 15 mins

Servings: 2

Ingredients:

- 1 teacup red or brown lentils, washed
- 1 tin (14 oz.) cubed tomatoes
- 1 onion, severed
- 2 pieces garlic, crushed
- 1 tsp paprika
- 1 tsp cumin
- 4 teacups low-sodium vegetable broth

Directions:

1. Sauté onion and garlic in the Instant Pot.
2. Include lentils, cubed tomatoes, spices, and vegetable broth.
3. Pressure cook for 10 mins.
4. Serve hot.

Per serving: Calories: 265kcal; Fat: 1gm; Carbs: 48gm; Protein: 17gm; Sugar: 4gm; Sodium: 350mg; Potassium: 655mg

192. Instant Pot Spinach and Mushroom Risotto

Preparation time: 10 mins

Cooking time: 10 mins

Servings: 2

Ingredients:

- 1 teacup Arborio rice
- 2 teacups low-sodium vegetable broth
- 1 teacup sliced mushrooms
- 2 teacups fresh spinach
- 1 onion, severed
- 2 pieces garlic, crushed

Directions:

1. Sauté onion and garlic in the Instant Pot.
2. Include Arborio rice then cook for 1 min.

3. Include mushrooms, spinach, and vegetable broth.
4. Pressure cook for 5 mins.
5. Stir well prior to serving.

Per serving: Calories: 324kcal; Fat: 1gm; Carbs: 72gm; Protein: 8gm; Sugar: 2gm; Sodium: 350mg; Potassium: 457mg

193. Instant Pot Mediterranean Quinoa Salad

Preparation time: 10 mins
Cooking time: 1 min
Servings: 2
Ingredients:

- 1 teacup quinoa, washed
- 1 teacup cubed cucumbers
- 1/2 teacup cubed tomatoes
- 1/4 teacup severed fresh parsley
- 2 tbsps lemon juice
- 2 tbsps olive oil
- 1 tsp dried oregano

Directions:

1. Blend quinoa & 2 teacups of water in the Instant Pot.
2. Pressure cook for 1 min.
3. Fluff quinoa with a fork then let it cool.
4. Mix in cucumbers, tomatoes, parsley, lemon juice, olive oil, and oregano.
5. Serve chilled.

Per serving: Calories: 385kcal; Fat: 14gm; Carbs: 54gm; Protein: 11gm; Sugar: 4gm; Sodium: 20mg; Potassium: 496mg

194. Instant Pot Sweet Potato and Lentil Stew

Preparation time: 15 mins
Cooking time: 10 mins
Servings: 2
Ingredients:

- 1 teacup red or brown lentils, washed
- 2 teacups cubed sweet potatoes
- 1 onion, severed
- 2 pieces garlic, crushed
- 1 tsp cumin
- 1 tsp paprika
- 4 teacups low-sodium vegetable broth

Directions:

1. Sauté onion and garlic in the Instant Pot.
2. Include lentils, sweet potatoes, spices, and vegetable broth.
3. Pressure cook for 5 mins.
4. Serve hot.

Per serving: Calories: 341kcal; Fat: 2gm; Carbs: 65gm; Protein: 20gm; Sugar: 7gm; Sodium: 350mg; Potassium: 347mg

195. Instant Pot Ratatouille

Preparation time: 15 mins
Cooking time: 5 mins

Servings: 2

Ingredients:

- 1 eggplant, cubed
- 2 zucchinis, cubed
- 1 bell pepper, cubed
- 1 onion, severed
- 2 pieces garlic, crushed
- 1 tin (14 oz.) cubed tomatoes
- 1 tsp dried thyme
- 1 tsp dried basil

Directions:

1. Sauté onion and garlic in the Instant Pot.
2. Include eggplant, zucchinis, bell pepper, cubed tomatoes, thyme, and basil.
3. Pressure cook for 2 mins.
4. Serve hot.

Per serving: Calories: 196kcal; Fat: 1gm; Carbs: 45gm; Protein: 7gm; Sugar: 15gm; Sodium: 370mg; Potassium: 525mg

196. Instant Pot Lemon Herb Rice with Asparagus

Preparation time: 10 mins

Cooking time: 1 min

Servings: 2

Ingredients:

- 1 teacup brown rice, washed
- 1 bunch asparagus, clipped then cut into 2-inch pieces
- 2 pieces garlic, crushed
- Zest and juice of 1 lemon
- 2 teacups low-sodium vegetable broth
- 1 tsp dried thyme
- 1 tsp dried rosemary

Directions:

1. Blend brown rice, asparagus, garlic, lemon zest, lemon juice, vegetable broth, thyme, and rosemary in the Instant Pot.
2. Pressure cook for 1 min.
3. Fluff rice with a fork prior to serving.

Per serving: Calories: 281kcal; Fat: 1gm; Carbs: 62gm; Protein: 7gm; Sugar: 2gm; Sodium: 300mg; Potassium: 452mg

197. Instant Pot Black Bean and Quinoa Stuffed Peppers

Preparation time: 15 mins

Cooking time: 5 mins

Servings: 2

Ingredients:

- 2 bell peppers, halved and seeded
- 1 teacup cooked quinoa
- 1 tin (15 oz.) black beans, that is drained and washed
- 1 teacup cubed tomatoes
- 1 tsp chili powder
- 1 tsp cumin

Directions:
1. Blend quinoa, black beans, cubed tomatoes, chili powder, and cumin inside your container.
2. Stuff bell pepper halves with the mixture.
3. Place stuffed peppers in the Instant Pot with 1 teacup of water.
4. Pressure cook for 5 mins.

Per serving: Calories: 337kcal; Fat: 2gm; Carbs: 65gm; Protein: 15gm; Sugar: 6gm; Sodium: 430mg; Potassium: 564mg

198. Instant Pot Cilantro Lime Rice with Black Beans

Preparation time: 10 mins
Cooking time: 1 min
Servings: 2
Ingredients:
- 1 teacup white rice, washed
- 1 tin (15 oz.) black beans, that is drained and washed
- Zest and juice of 1 lime
- 2 tbsps fresh cilantro, severed
- 2 teacups low-sodium vegetable broth

Directions:
1. Blend white rice, black beans, lime zest, lime juice, cilantro, and vegetable broth in the Instant Pot.
2. Pressure cook for 1 min.
3. Fluff rice with a fork prior to serving.

Per serving: Calories: 311kcal; Fat: 1gm; Carbs: 65gm; Protein: 10gm; Sugar: 2gm; Sodium: 400mg; Potassium: 420mg

199. Instant Pot Butternut Squash Soup

Preparation time: 10 mins
Cooking time: 10 mins
Servings: 2
Ingredients:
- 2 teacups cubed butternut squash
- 1 onion, severed
- 2 pieces garlic, crushed
- 1 tsp dried sage
- 4 teacups low-sodium vegetable broth

Directions:
1. Sauté onion and garlic in the Instant Pot.
2. Include butternut squash, dried sage, and vegetable broth.
3. Pressure cook for 5 mins.
4. Blend till smooth prior to serving.

Per serving: Calories: 186kcal; Fat: 1gm; Carbs: 44gm; Protein: 3gm; Sugar: 5gm; Sodium: 340mg; Potassium: 603mg

200. Instant Pot Mexican Rice with Pinto Beans

Preparation time: 10 mins
Cooking time: 1 min
Servings: 2

Ingredients:

- 1 teacup white rice, washed
- 1 teacup cooked pinto beans
- 1 teacup cubed tomatoes
- 1/2 teacup cubed onions
- 1/2 teacup cubed bell peppers
- 1 tsp chili powder
- 1 tsp cumin
- 2 teacups low-sodium vegetable broth

Directions:

1. Blend white rice, pinto beans, cubed tomatoes, onions, bell peppers, chili powder, cumin, and vegetable broth in the Instant Pot.
2. Pressure cook for 1 min.
3. Fluff rice with a fork prior to serving.

Per serving: Calories: 321kcal; Fat: 2gm; Carbs: 70gm; Protein: 8gm; Sugar: 5gm; Sodium: 300mg; Potassium: 493mg

CHAPTER 15. BONUS #2 EASY AND DELICIOUS MEAL PREPS FOR VERY BUSY PEOPLE WHO ARE OFTEN OUT FOR WORK

201. Quinoa and Vegetable Stir-Fry

Preparation time: 15 mins
Cooking time: 20 mins
Servings: 2

Ingredients:

- 1 teacup quinoa
- 2 teacups mixed vegetables (broccoli, bell peppers, carrots)
- 2 pieces garlic, crushed
- Low-sodium soy sauce

Directions:

1. Cook quinoa according to package instructions.
2. Stir-fry vegetables and garlic in your non-stick pan.
3. Toss cooked quinoa into the pan and include soy sauce.

Per serving: Calories: 307kcal; Fat: 2gm; Carbs: 60gm; Protein: 10gm; Sugar: 4gm; Sodium: 150mg; Potassium: 401mg

202. Chickpea and Spinach Curry

Preparation time: 15 mins
Cooking time: 25 mins
Servings: 2

Ingredients:

- 1 tin chickpeas, that is drained and washed
- 2 teacups fresh spinach
- 1 onion, severed
- 1 tsp curry powder

Directions:

1. Sauté onions till translucent.
2. Include chickpeas, spinach, and curry powder.
3. Cook till spinach wilts.

Per serving: Calories: 308kcal; Fat: 2gm; Carbs: 60gm; Protein: 15gm; Sugar: 5gm; Sodium: 150mg; Potassium: 608mg

203. Spinach and Mushroom Frittata

Preparation time: 10 mins
Cooking time: 20 mins
Servings: 2

Ingredients:

- 4 eggs
- 1 teacup spinach leaves
- 1 teacup sliced mushrooms
- 1/2 tsp black pepper

Directions:

1. Whisk eggs and black pepper inside your container.

2. Sauté spinach and mushrooms in your non-stick pan till wilted.
3. Pour egg mixture over vegetables then cook till set.

Per serving: Calories: 25kcal; Fat: 10gm; Carbs: 10gm; Protein: 15gm; Sugar: 2gm; Sodium: 100mg; Potassium: 453mg

204. Cauliflower Rice Bowl

Preparation time: 15 mins
Cooking time: 15 mins
Servings: 2
Ingredients:

- 2 teacups cauliflower rice (store-bought or homemade)
- 1 teacup cubed mixed vegetables (bell peppers, carrots, peas)
- 1/2 tsp garlic powder
- Low-sodium soy sauce

Directions:

1. Sauté mixed vegetables and garlic powder till tender.
2. Include cauliflower rice and stir-fry.
3. Spray with low-sodium soy sauce.

Per serving: Calories: 156kcal; Fat: 1gm; Carbs: 30gm; Protein: 7gm; Sugar: 8gm; Sodium: 100mg; Potassium: 453mg

205. Salmon and Asparagus Foil Pack

Preparation time: 10 mins
Cooking time: 20 mins
Servings: 2
Ingredients:

- 2 salmon fillets
- 1 teacup asparagus spears
- Lemon slices
- Fresh dill

Directions:

1. Place salmon fillets and asparagus on separate sheets of aluminum foil.
2. Top with lemon slices and fresh dill.
3. Seal the foil into packets then bake at 375 deg.F for 20 mins.

Per serving: Calories: 305kcal; Fat: 15gm; Carbs: 10gm; Protein: 30gm; Sugar: 5gm; Sodium: 50mg; Potassium: 689mg

206. Eggplant and Chickpea Curry

Preparation time: 15 mins
Cooking time: 25 mins
Servings: 2
Ingredients:

- 1 small eggplant, cubed
- 1 tin chickpeas, drained
- 1 onion, severed
- 2 pieces garlic, crushed
- 1 tsp curry powder

Directions:

1. Sauté onion and garlic till softened.

2. Include eggplant, chickpeas, and curry powder. Cook till eggplant is tender.
3. Serve over brown rice.

Per serving: Calories: 281kcal; Fat: 1gm; Carbs: 60gm; Protein: 10gm; Sugar: 6gm; Sodium: 150mg; Potassium: 553mg

207. Spaghetti Squash with Tomato Sauce

Preparation time: 15 mins
Cooking time: 45 mins
Servings: 2
Ingredients:

- 1 spaghetti squash
- 1 tin cubed tomatoes (no added salt)
- 1 tsp Italian seasoning
- Fresh basil leaves

Directions:

1. Cut spaghetti squash in ½, remove seeds, and roast in the oven till tender.
2. Heat cubed tomatoes with Italian seasoning.
3. Scrape the squash into "noodles" and serve with tomato sauce.

Per serving: Calories: 151kcal; Fat: 1gm; Carbs: 35gm; Protein: 3gm; Sugar: 10gm; Sodium: 50mg; Potassium: 563mg

208. Mushroom and Spinach Stuffed Bell Peppers

Preparation time: 20 mins
Cooking time: 40 mins
Servings: 2
Ingredients:

- 2 bell peppers, halved and seeded
- 2 teacups mushrooms, severed
- 2 teacups fresh spinach
- 1 tsp garlic powder

Directions:

1. Sauté mushrooms and spinach with garlic powder till wilted.
2. Fill bell pepper halves with the mixture.
3. Bake for 40 mins.

Per serving: Calories: 202kcal; Fat: 2gm; Carbs: 40gm; Protein: 10gm; Sugar: 10gm; Sodium: 50mg; Potassium: 686mg

209. Roasted Vegetable and Quinoa Bowl

Preparation time: 15 mins
Cooking time: 30 mins
Servings: 2
Ingredients:

- 2 teacups mixed roasted vegetables (zucchini, bell peppers, cherry tomatoes)
- 1 teacup cooked quinoa

- Balsamic vinaigrette dressing (low-sodium)
- Fresh basil leaves

Directions:
1. Roast vegetables in the oven till tender.
2. Serve over quinoa then spray with balsamic vinaigrette.
3. Garnish with fresh basil leaves.

Per serving: Calories: 258kcal; Fat: 2gm; Carbs: 50gm; Protein: 7gm; Sugar: 5gm; Sodium: 50mg; Potassium: 637mg

210. Chickpea and Vegetable Stir-Fry

Preparation time: 15 mins
Cooking time: 20 mins
Servings: 2
Ingredients:

- 1 tin chickpeas, that is drained and washed
- 2 teacups mixed vegetables (snow peas, bell peppers, broccoli)
- 2 pieces garlic, crushed
- Low-sodium soy sauce

Directions:
1. Stir-fry mixed vegetables and garlic in your non-stick pan.
2. Include chickpeas and a splash of low-sodium soy sauce.
3. Cook till vegetables are tender.

Per serving: Calories: 304kcal; Fat: 2gm; Carbs: 60gm; Protein: 12gm; Sugar: 6gm; Sodium: 200mg; Potassium: 451mg

211. Cucumber and Tomato Salad

Preparation time: 10 mins
Cooking time: 0 mins (no cooking required)
Servings: 2
Ingredients:

- 1 cucumber, sliced
- 2 tomatoes, cubed
- Red onion, finely cut
- Fresh parsley
- Balsamic vinegar (low-sodium)

Directions:
1. Blend cucumber, tomatoes, and red onion inside your container.
2. Sprinkle with fresh parsley then spray with low-sodium balsamic vinegar.

Per serving: Calories: 85kcal; Fat: 1gm; Carbs: 20gm; Protein: 2gm; Sugar: 10gm; Sodium: 10mg; Potassium: 563mg

212. Sweet Potato and Black Bean Hash

Preparation time: 15 mins
Cooking time: 20 mins
Servings: 2
Ingredients:

- 2 teacups sweet potatoes, cubed

- 1 tin black beans, that is drained and washed
- 1 red bell pepper, cubed
- 1 tsp paprika

Directions:
1. Sauté sweet potatoes and red bell pepper till tender.
2. Include black beans and paprika. Cook till heated through.

Per serving: Calories: 251kcal; Fat: 1gm; Carbs: 50gm; Protein: 10gm; Sugar: 8gm; Sodium: 150mg; Potassium: 634mg

213. Mango and Black Bean Salad

Preparation time: 15 mins
Cooking time: 0 mins (no cooking required)
Servings: 2
Ingredients:

- 1 tin black beans, that is drained and washed
- 1 ripe mango, cubed
- Red bell pepper, cubed
- Fresh cilantro
- Lime juice

Directions:
1. Blend black beans, mango, and red bell pepper inside your container.
2. Garnish with fresh cilantro then spray with lime juice.

Per serving: Calories: 253kcal; Fat: 1gm; Carbs: 50gm; Protein: 10gm; Sugar: 18gm; Sodium: 10mg; Potassium: 593mg

214. Tofu and Vegetable Stir-Fry

Preparation time: 15 mins
Cooking time: 20 mins
Servings: 2
Ingredients:

- 8 oz. firm tofu, cubed
- 2 teacups mixed vegetables (broccoli, snap peas, carrots)
- Low-sodium stir-fry sauce
- Sesame seeds (optional)

Directions:
1. Sauté tofu till golden brown.
2. Include mixed vegetables and stir-fry till tender.
3. Toss with low-sodium stir-fry sauce then spray with sesame seeds if anticipated.

Per serving: Calories: 255kcal; Fat: 10gm; Carbs: 20gm; Protein: 18gm; Sugar: 8gm; Sodium: 200mg; Potassium: 439mg

215. Cauliflower and Broccoli Salad

Preparation time: 15 mins
Cooking time: 5 mins
Servings: 2

Ingredients:
- 2 teacups cauliflower florets
- 2 teacups broccoli florets
- Red onion, finely cut
- Dijon mustard vinaigrette (low-sodium)
- Fresh parsley

Directions:
1. Steam cauliflower and broccoli till tender.
2. Toss with finely cut red onion then spray with Dijon mustard vinaigrette.
3. Garnish with fresh parsley.

Per serving: Calories: 157kcal; Fat: 1gm; Carbs: 30gm; Protein: 8gm; Sugar: 10gm; Sodium: 102mg; Potassium: 638mg

216. Mushroom and Spinach Omelet

Preparation time: 10 mins
Cooking time: 10 mins
Servings: 2
Ingredients:
- 4 eggs
- 2 teacups fresh spinach
- 1 teacup sliced mushrooms
- Black pepper

Directions:
1. Whisk eggs and black pepper inside your container.
2. Sauté mushrooms till soft, then include spinach then cook till wilted.
3. Transfer the egg mixture over the veggies then cook till set.

Per serving: Calories: 201kcal; Fat: 10gm; Carbs: 5gm; Protein: 16gm; Sugar: 2gm; Sodium: 156mg; Potassium: 539mg

217. Tofu and Vegetable Curry

Preparation time: 15 mins
Cooking time: 25 mins
Servings: 2
Ingredients:
- 8 oz. firm tofu, cubed
- 2 teacups mixed vegetables (bell peppers, peas, carrots)
- 2 tbsps curry powder
- Coconut milk (unsweetened)

Directions:
1. Sauté tofu till golden brown.
2. Include mixed vegetables then cook till tender.
3. Stir in curry powder and enough coconut milk to create a creamy sauce.

Per serving: Calories: 303kcal; Fat: 15gm; Carbs: 30gm; Protein: 18gm; Sugar: 8gm; Sodium: 150mg; Potassium: 539mg

218. Lemon Garlic Roasted Brussels Sprouts

Preparation time: 10 mins
Cooking time: 25 mins
Servings: 2
Ingredients:

- 2 teacups Brussels sprouts, halved
- 2 pieces garlic, crushed
- Zest and juice of 1 lemon
- Olive oil (optional)

Directions:

1. Toss Brussels sprouts with garlic, lemon zest, and juice.
2. Optionally, spray using a small amount of olive oil.
3. Roast in the oven till tender.

Per serving: Calories: 108kcal; Fat: 2gm; Carbs: 20gm; Protein: 5gm; Sugar: 4gm; Sodium: 20mg; Potassium: 586mg

219. Cabbage and Carrot Slaw

Preparation time: 15 mins
Cooking time: 0 mins (no cooking required)
Servings: 2
Ingredients:

- 2 teacups shredded cabbage
- 1 teacup grated carrots
- Greek yogurt (plain, low-fat)
- Apple cider vinegar
- Dijon mustard

Directions:

1. Blend shredded cabbage and grated carrots inside your container.
2. Inside your distinct container, mix Greek yogurt, apple cider vinegar, and Dijon mustard for the dressing.
3. Toss the slaw with the dressing.

Per serving: Calories: 75kcal; Fat: 1gm; Carbs: 15gm; Protein: 3gm; Sugar: 8gm; Sodium: 66mg; Potassium: 358mg

220. Baked Sweet Potatoes with Salsa

Preparation time: 10 mins
Cooking time: 45 mins
Servings: 2
Ingredients:

- 2 medium sweet potatoes
- Homemade or store-bought salsa (no added sugar)
- Fresh cilantro

Directions:

1. Pierce sweet potatoes with a fork then bake in the oven till tender.
2. Top with salsa and garnish with fresh cilantro.

Per serving: Calories: 201kcal; Fat: 1gm; Carbs: 45gm; Protein: 4gm; Sugar: 15gm; Sodium: 352mg; Potassium: 538mg

30-DAY MEAL PLAN

Day	Breakfast	Morning Snacks	Lunch	Afternoon Snacks	Dinner
1	Berry and Spinach Smoothie	Mango and Coconut Chia Pudding	Teriyaki Chicken with Broccoli	Hummus and Veggie Sticks	Beef and Green Bean Stir-Fry
2	Almond and Banana Toast	Crispy Baked Zucchini Chips	Beef and Spinach Stuffed Portobello Mushrooms	Edamame with Lemon and Sea Salt	Lemon Dill Baked Catfish
3	Mixed Berry Smoothie	Chia Pudding with Berries	Quinoa-Stuffed Bell Peppers	Watermelon and Mint Skewers	Tomato Basil Chicken
4	Quinoa Breakfast Bowl	Tuna and Cucumber Boats	Brown Rice and Vegetable Stir-Fry	Bell Pepper and Guacamole Bites	Baked Herb-Crusted Snapper
5	Veggie Breakfast Burrito	Cauliflower Popcorn	Herbed Chicken Stir-Fry	Avocado and Salsa Dip	Ginger Sesame Chicken Stir-Fry
6	Peanut Butter and Banana Oatmeal	Hard-Boiled Eggs with Mustard	Beef and Mushroom Lettuce Wraps	Cherry Tomatoes with Balsamic Glaze	Garlic and Herb Baked Scallops
7	Sweet Potato and Spinach Hash	Quinoa Salad	Pineapple Teriyaki Chicken	Spinach and Tomato Frittata	Beef and Pea Risotto
8	Blueberry and Almond Overnight Oats	Mango and Coconut Chia Pudding	Grilled Tuna Steak with Cucumber Salad	Crispy Baked Zucchini Chips	Grilled Swordfish with Herb Salsa

9	Raspberry and Almond Chia Pudding	Watermelon and Mint Skewers	Teriyaki Chicken with Broccoli	Edamame with Lemon and Sea Salt	Roasted Veggie and Chickpea Bowl
10	Veggie and Hummus Wrap	Hummus and Veggie Sticks	Mediterranean Style Grilled Sardines	Chia Pudding with Berries	Quinoa and Asparagus Salad
11	Tomato and Basil Omelet	Chia Pudding with Berries	Tomato Basil Chicken	Bell Pepper and Guacamole Bites	Beef and Tomato Quinoa Bowl
12	Cinnamon and Apple Oatmeal	Crispy Baked Zucchini Chips	Beef and Spinach Stuffed Portobello Mushrooms	Edamame with Lemon and Sea Salt	Beef and Mushroom Lettuce Wraps
13	Veggie and Quinoa Breakfast Bowl	Quinoa Salad	Beef and Green Bean Stir-Fry	Watermelon and Mint Skewers	Baked Salmon with Dill
14	Oatmeal with Mixed Berries	Hard-Boiled Eggs with Mustard	Herb-Crusted Chicken with Sautéed Spinach	Spinach and Tomato Frittata	Beef and Cauliflower Rice Bowl
15	Almond and Banana Toast	Avocado and Salsa Dip	Curry Chicken with Cauliflower Rice	Cherry Tomatoes with Balsamic Glaze	Lentil and Vegetable Soup
16	Quinoa Breakfast Bowl	Mango and Coconut Chia Pudding	Beef and Mushroom Lettuce Wraps	Hummus and Veggie Sticks	Mushroom and Spinach Risotto
17	Tofu Scramble	Watermelon and Mint Skewers	Spaghetti Squash Primavera	Crispy Baked Zucchini Chips	Millet and Roasted

					Vegetable Salad
18	Oatmeal with Mixed Berries	Chia Pudding with Berries	Baked Garlic Butter Shrimp	Bell Pepper and Guacamole Bites	Baked Herb-Crusted Turkey Breast
19	Mixed Berry Smoothie	Hard-Boiled Eggs with Mustard	Beef and Asparagus Stir-Fry	Edamame with Lemon and Sea Salt	Garlic and Herb Baked Scallops
20	Berry and Spinach Smoothie	Crispy Baked Zucchini Chips	Beef and Tomato Quinoa Bowl	Mango and Coconut Chia Pudding	Beef and Vegetable Kabobs
21	Quinoa Breakfast Bowl	Hummus and Veggie Sticks	Beef and Pea Risotto	Cherry Tomatoes with Balsamic Glaze	Stuffed Portobello Mushrooms
22	Tomato and Basil Omelet	Avocado and Salsa Dip	Almond-Crusted Chicken Tenders	Watermelon and Mint Skewers	Beef and Spinach Stuffed Portobello Mushrooms
23	Veggie Breakfast Burrito	Cauliflower Popcorn	Paprika Chicken with Roasted Vegetables	Spinach and Tomato Frittata	Rosemary Dijon Chicken
24	Peanut Butter and Banana Oatmeal	Quinoa Salad	Beef and Cauliflower Rice Bowl	Edamame with Lemon and Sea Salt	Baked Lemon Garlic Tilapia
25	Blueberry and Almond Overnight Oats	Mango and Coconut Chia Pudding	Citrus-Marinated Grilled Chicken	Bell Pepper and Guacamole Bites	Beef and Sweet Potato Hash

26	Raspberry and Almond Chia Pudding	Watermelon and Mint Skewers	Spicy Cajun Chicken with Sautéed Spinach	Chia Pudding with Berries	Ginger Sesame Chicken Stir-Fry
27	Veggie and Hummus Wrap	Hard-Boiled Eggs with Mustard	Herb-Crusted Chicken with Sautéed Spinach	Hummus and Veggie Sticks	Cilantro Lime Chicken Tenders
28	Cinnamon and Apple Oatmeal	Crispy Baked Zucchini Chips	Beef and Mushroom Lettuce Wraps	Cherry Tomatoes with Balsamic Glaze	Beef and Green Bean Stir-Fry
29	Sweet Potato and Spinach Hash	Chia Pudding with Berries	Sesame Crusted Salmon with Spinach	Edamame with Lemon and Sea Salt	Broiled Lemon Butter Lobster Tails
30	Veggie and Quinoa Breakfast Bowl	Hummus and Veggie Sticks	Honey Mustard Chicken with Steamed Asparagus	Spinach and Tomato Frittata	Shrimp and Vegetable Stir-Fry

CONCLUSION

In conclusion, the DASH diet stands as a firmly established and remarkably efficient dietary regimen, bringing forth a multitude of health advantages. Grounded in the principles of balanced nutrition, it places a strong emphasis on the inclusion of vegetables, fruits, whole grains, lean proteins, and low-fat dairy items, all the while advocating for the reduction of sodium and saturated fat intake. Scientific evidence supports that the DASH diet can effectively lower blood pressure, mitigate the likelihood of heart disease, and foster overall well-being.

By following the principles of the DASH diet, individuals can not only improve their cardiovascular health but also manage their weight, lower cholesterol levels, and enhance their overall quality of life. Its flexibility allows for customization to personal tastes and dietary preferences, making it a sustainable and enjoyable lifestyle choice.

If you're looking to adopt a healthier eating pattern and experience the numerous benefits of the DASH diet, I encourage you to explore the recipes and meal plan contained within the book. By trying out these delicious and nutritious dishes, you'll embark on a journey toward better health and well-being. Remember that small, consistent changes in your diet can lead to significant improvements in your health over time. So, don't hesitate to give it a try – your body and future self will thank you for it!

MEASUREMENT CONVERSION CHART

Volume Equivalents (Liquid)

US Standard	US Standard (oz.)	Metric (approximate)
2 tbsps	1 fl. oz.	30 milliliter
¼ teacup	2 fl. oz.	60 milliliter
½ teacup	4 fl. oz.	120 milliliter
1 teacup	8 fl. oz.	240 milliliter
1½ teacups	12 fl. oz.	355 milliliter
2 teacups or 1 pint	16 fl. oz.	475 milliliter
4 teacups or 1 quart	32 fl. oz.	1 Liter
1 gallon	128 fl. oz.	4 Liter

Volume Equivalents (Dry)

US Standard	Metric (approximate)
⅛ tsp	0.5 milliliter
¼ tsp	1 milliliter
½ tsp	2 milliliter
¾ tsp	4 milliliter
1 tsp	5 milliliter
1 tbsp	15 milliliter
¼ teacup	59 milliliter
⅓ teacup	79 milliliter
½ teacup	118 milliliter
⅔ teacup	156 milliliter
¾ teacup	177 milliliter
1 teacup	235 milliliter
2 teacups or 1 pint	475 milliliter
3 teacups	700 milliliter

| 4 teacups or 1 quart | 1 Liter |

Oven Temperatures

Fahrenheit (F)	Celsius (C) (approximate)
250 deg.F	120 deg.C
300 deg.F	150 deg.C
325 deg.F	165 deg.C
350 deg.F	180 deg.C
375 deg.F	190 deg.C
400 deg.F	200 deg.C
425 deg.F	220 deg.C
450 deg.F	230 deg.C

Weight Equivalents

US Standard	Metric (approximate)
1 tbsp	15 gm
½ oz.	15 gm
1 oz.	30 gm
2 oz.	60 gm
4 oz.	115 gm
8 oz.	225 gm
12 oz.	340 gm
16 oz. or 1 lb.	455 gm

INDEX

Almond and Banana Toast; 26
Almond-Crusted Chicken Tenders; 56
Apricot and Almond Rice Pudding; 94
Artichoke and Spinach Soup; 91
Asian-Inspired Edamame Salad; 45
Asparagus and Lemon Soup; 87
Avocado and Salsa Dip; 33
Avocado and Tomato Salad; 85
Avocado Kale Smoothie; 29
Baked Apples with Cinnamon; 92
Baked Banana with Cinnamon and Walnuts; 95
Baked Coconut Shrimp; 78
Baked Garlic Butter Shrimp; 76
Baked Herb-Crusted Snapper; 73
Baked Herb-Crusted Turkey Breast; 52
Baked Lemon Garlic Tilapia; 75
Baked Salmon with Dill; 73
Baked Sweet Potatoes with Salsa; 115
Balsamic Dijon Vinaigrette; 40
Banana Kiwi Smoothie; 31
Basil Tomato Sauce; 42
Beef and Asparagus Stir-Fry; 59
Beef and Bean Chili; 60
Beef and Cauliflower Rice Bowl; 64
Beef and Cucumber Salad; 63
Beef and Eggplant Skillet; 61
Beef and Green Bean Stir-Fry; 61
Beef and Mushroom Lettuce Wraps; 62
Beef and Mushroom Stuffed Bell Peppers; 59
Beef and Pea Risotto; 62
Beef and Spinach Salad; 59
Beef and Spinach Stuffed Portobello Mushrooms; 60
Beef and Sweet Potato Hash; 63
Beef and Tomato Quinoa Bowl; 64
Beef and Vegetable Kabobs; 58
Beef Stir-Fry with Broccoli and Bell Peppers; 58
Bell Pepper and Guacamole Bites; 35
Berry and Spinach Smoothie; 21
Berry Blast Smoothie; 27
Black Bean and Corn Salad; 46
Blueberry and Almond Overnight Oats; 23
Blueberry Chia Seed Shake; 31
Broccoli and Chickpea Salad with Lemon Garlic Dressing; 51
Broccoli and White Bean Soup; 87
Broiled Lemon Butter Lobster Tails; 77
Brown Rice and Vegetable Stir-Fry; 67
Brown Rice Pilaf; 81
Cabbage and Black Bean Tacos; 70
Cabbage and Carrot Slaw; 114
Caprese Salad with Balsamic Glaze; 47
Carrot and Ginger Soup; 90
Carrot Cake Smoothie; 28
Cauliflower "Mashed Potatoes"; 84
Cauliflower and Broccoli Salad; 113
Cauliflower and Chickpea Curry; 68
Cauliflower and Turmeric Soup; 88
Cauliflower Popcorn; 37
Cauliflower Rice Bowl; 109
Cherry Almond Smoothie; 29
Cherry Tomatoes with Balsamic Glaze; 34
Chia Pudding with Berries; 38
Chickpea and Spinach Curry; 108
Chickpea and Vegetable Soup; 86
Chickpea and Vegetable Stir-Fry; 111
Chili-Lime Seasoning; 40
Chocolate Avocado Mousse; 92
Cilantro Lime Chicken Tenders; 53
Cinnamon and Apple Oatmeal; 25
Cinnamon Apple Smoothie; 28
Cinnamon Baked Pears; 93
Citrus Kale Smoothie; 28
Citrus-Marinated Grilled Chicken; 52
Coconut and Mango Chia Popsicles; 95
Cranberry and Walnut Quinoa; 96
Crispy Baked Zucchini Chips; 36
Cucumber and Tomato Salad; 111
Cumin-Lime Dressing; 42
Curry Chicken with Cauliflower Rice; 55
Edamame with Lemon and Sea Salt; 33
Eggplant and Chickpea Curry; 109
Eggplant and Tomato Soup; 90
Frozen Yogurt Bark; 95

Fruit Salad with Honey-Lime Drizzle; 93
Garlic and Herb Baked Scallops; 74
Garlic and Herb Seasoning; 39
Garlic Roasted Brussels Sprouts; 80
Ginger Sesame Chicken Stir-Fry; 53
Ginger Sesame Dressing; 39
Greek Salad; 68
Green Bean and Almond Soup; 91
Green Pea and Mint Soup; 89
Green Power Smoothie; 27
Grilled Eggplant; 83
Grilled Swordfish with Herb Salsa; 74
Grilled Tuna Steak with Cucumber Salad; 76
Grilled Vegetable Salad; 34
Hard-Boiled Eggs with Mustard; 35
Herb-Crusted Chicken with Sautéed Spinach; 56
Herbed Brown Lentils; 82
Herbed Chicken Stir-Fry; 52
Honey Mustard Chicken with Steamed Asparagus; 54
Hummus and Veggie Sticks; 33
Instant Pot Black Bean and Corn Soup; 102
Instant Pot Black Bean and Quinoa Stuffed Peppers; 105
Instant Pot Black-Eyed Pea Stew; 99
Instant Pot Brown Rice and Bean Bowl; 100
Instant Pot Butternut Squash Soup; 106
Instant Pot Chickpea Curry; 98
Instant Pot Cilantro Lime Rice with Black Beans; 106
Instant Pot Lemon Herb Rice with Asparagus; 105
Instant Pot Mediterranean Quinoa Salad; 103
Instant Pot Mexican Rice with Pinto Beans; 106
Instant Pot Minestrone Soup; 98
Instant Pot Moroccan Chickpea Stew; 100
Instant Pot Quinoa and Black Bean Bowl; 98
Instant Pot Ratatouille; 104
Instant Pot Red Lentil Curry; 99
Instant Pot Spinach and Lentil Curry; 101
Instant Pot Spinach and Mushroom Risotto; 103
Instant Pot Sweet Potato and Lentil Stew; 104
Instant Pot Tomato and Lentil Soup; 102
Instant Pot Vegetable and Chickpea Curry; 101
Lemon Basil Pesto; 41
Lemon Dill Baked Catfish; 75
Lemon Dill Dressing; 42
Lemon Garlic Roasted Brussels Sprouts; 114
Lemon Herb Quinoa; 80
Lemon Herb Quinoa Salad; 44
Lemon Herb Sauce; 39
Lemon Pepper Seasoning; 41
Lentil and Vegetable Soup; 65
Mango and Black Bean Salad; 112
Mango and Coconut Chia Pudding; 36
Mango and Raspberry Frozen Yogurt; 93
Mango Spinach Smoothie; 30
Mediterranean Chickpea Salad; 48
Mediterranean Herb Blend; 43
Mediterranean Lentil Salad; 44
Mediterranean Style Grilled Sardines; 77
Millet and Roasted Vegetable Salad; 72
Minty Watermelon Slush; 96
Mixed Berry Smoothie; 25
Mushroom and Spinach Omelet; 113
Mushroom and Spinach Risotto; 66
Mushroom and Spinach Stuffed Bell Peppers; 110
Oatmeal with Mixed Berries; 21
Paprika Chicken with Roasted Vegetables; 54
Peach Almond Smoothie; 30
Peach and Blueberry Crisp; 94
Peach and Raspberry Smoothie; 97
Peanut Butter and Banana Oatmeal; 23
Pineapple and Banana Sorbet; 92
Pineapple Teriyaki Chicken; 57
Poached Tilapia with Herbed Tomatoes; 73
Pomegranate and Kiwi Fruit Salad; 96
Pomegranate Blueberry Shake; 29
Quinoa and Asparagus Salad; 71
Quinoa and Vegetable Stir-Fry; 108
Quinoa Breakfast Bowl; 21
Quinoa Salad; 37
Quinoa-Stuffed Bell Peppers; 65
Raspberry and Almond Chia Pudding; 24
Raspberry Oatmeal Smoothie; 30
Roasted Asparagus; 80
Roasted Beet and Orange Salad; 50
Roasted Cauliflower with Turmeric; 85
Roasted Red Pepper Hummus; 83
Roasted Sweet Potato and Kale Salad; 49
Roasted Vegetable and Quinoa Bowl; 111
Roasted Veggie and Chickpea Bowl; 66
Rosemary Dijon Chicken; 53

Rosemary Dijon Marinade; 41
Salmon and Asparagus Foil Pack; 109
Sautéed Snow Peas with Lemon; 83
Sautéed Spinach with Garlic; 82
Sautéed Swiss Chard; 84
Seared Scallops with Spinach; 78
Sesame Crusted Salmon with Spinach; 77
Sesame Ginger Sauce; 43
Shrimp and Vegetable Stir-Fry; 75
Spaghetti Squash Primavera; 69
Spaghetti Squash with Tomato Sauce; 110
Spicy Bell Pepper Soup; 90
Spicy Cajun Chicken with Sautéed Spinach; 57
Spicy Tomato Salsa; 41
Spinach and Avocado Salad with Cilantro Lime Dressing; 48
Spinach and Chickpea Salad with Lemon Tahini Dressing; 47
Spinach and Mushroom Frittata; 108
Spinach and Mushroom Oatmeal; 67
Spinach and Mushroom Soup; 87
Spinach and Pear Salad with Dijon Vinaigrette; 50
Spinach and Pineapple Smoothie; 31
Spinach and Red Lentil Soup; 89
Spinach and Strawberry Salad; 46
Spinach and Tomato Frittata; 34

Steamed Green Beans with Almonds; 81
Stir-Fried Broccoli and Mushrooms; 82
Stuffed Portobello Mushrooms; 71
Sweet Potato and Black Bean Hash; 112
Sweet Potato and Black Bean Soup; 88
Sweet Potato and Chickpea Hash; 70
Sweet Potato and Spinach Hash; 22
Teriyaki Chicken with Broccoli; 56
Tofu and Vegetable Curry; 114
Tofu and Vegetable Stir-Fry; 112
Tofu Scramble; 23
Tomato and Basil Omelet; 26
Tomato Basil Chicken; 55
Tropical Delight Smoothie; 27
Tuna and Cucumber Boats; 36
Tuna and White Bean Salad; 45
Turmeric and Cumin Seasoning; 40
Vegetable Quinoa Soup; 86
Veggie and Hummus Wrap; 24
Veggie and Quinoa Breakfast Bowl; 25
Veggie Breakfast Burrito; 22
Waldorf Salad with Greek Yogurt Dressing; 49
Watermelon and Mint Skewers; 37
Zucchini and Basil Soup; 89
Zucchini Noodles with Tomato Sauce; 69

HERE IS YOUR TWO AMAZING *EXTRA BONUSES*!

#1 "The Delicious Mediterranean DASH Diet Cookbook"

Combining the DASH Diet and the Mediterranean Diet, two top diets for great health, this cookbook is your ticket to better health with yumminess included. It is full of easy recipes that follow these diets to help you lower your blood pressure and stay healthy while enjoying great taste and easy cooking. You will discover 180 made easy with tasty recipes perfect for beginners: breakfasts, soups, salads, main dishes, snack and desserts made with easy-to-find and natural ingredients from your local supermarket.

CLICK HERE TO DOWNLOAD THE EBOOK FOR FREE
or
SCAN HERE TO DOWNLOAD THE EBOOK FOR FREE

#2 Daily Routine of Somatic Exercises with Explanations and Images

To reduce stress, muscle tension, cortisol levels and blood pressure it is crucial to undertake targeted actions to achieve integrated well-being of the body and mind. In addition to following a healthy and balanced diet, it is necessary to maintain the habit of exercising every day. Somatic exercises play a crucial role in this process. Through daily routines of these activities, we can establish a positive connection with our emotions and our body. This practice not only promotes a sense of overall well-being and greater self-awareness but also contributes to increasing mental clarity. The controlled and conscious movements of Somatic Exercises help to release accumulated tensions and realign the body with the mind, offering a simple and enjoyable way to face daily stress more effectively and healthily.

CLICK HERE TO DOWNLOAD THE BONUS FOR FREE
or
SCAN HERE TO DOWNLOAD THE BONUS FOR FREE

Printed in Great Britain
by Amazon